Relation*Shift*

REVOLUTIONARY
FUNDRAISING

*by Michael Bassoff
and Steve Chandler*

Robert D. Reed Publishers
P.O. Box 1992
Bandon, OR 97411
(541) 347-9882; Fax: -9883
4bobreed@msn.com
www.rdrpublishers.com

Designed and typeset by Katherine Hyde
Cover designed by Julia A. Gaskill at Graphics Plus

ISBN 1-885003-93-5

Library of Congress Control Number: 2001090962

Produced and Printed in the United States of America

*Dedicated to the memory of
Willie Bassoff and
Peg Chandler*

Acknowledgments

We are grateful to: Kathryn Eimers for her editing and encouragement; Alison Bassoff; Dr. Sydney E. Salmon; Richard Imwalle; Jeff Covey; Howard Covey; Jessica Neuhoff; Mary Popovich; Darrell Price; Debra Bowles; The Arizona Cancer Center; The Green Valley Associates in Cancer Research; Milt Stamatis; Terry Hill; Miranda Lee; Paul Frank; Larry Smith; and Fredric O. Knipe III.

Contents

1	Introduction	Let There Be a Shift

FUNDRAISING'S 20 MOST DAMAGING MYTHS

4	MYTH #1	You Are Robin Hood
14	MYTH #2	Fundraising Is a Science
22	MYTH #3	Planned Gifts Depend on Death
26	MYTH #4	A Down Economy Is Bad for Fundraising
32	MYTH #5	It's All in Who You Know
36	MYTH #6	You've Got To Get the Word Out
54	MYTH #7	Only Rich People Can Help You
58	MYTH #8	Don't Waste Time on Lawyers and Accountants
60	MYTH #9	Big Money Comes from Big Companies
62	MYTH #10	You Need a Bigger Staff
66	MYTH #11	You Should Keep Your Communications Simple
72	MYTH #12	Only the Rich Should Talk to the Rich
76	MYTH #13	Giving Is Purely Emotional
80	MYTH #14	Your Board Is Undermotivated
86	MYTH #15	You Shouldn't Appear To Be Too Successful
90	MYTH #16	You Need a System for Recognizing Donors
94	MYTH #17	You Need Special Events
100	MYTH #18	Your Organization Is Too Unusual
104	MYTH #19	It Takes Money To Raise Money
110	MYTH #20	Fundraising Is a Frustrating Job
115	Shift Work	So What Do You Do Now?
120	About the Authors	

The deepest principle in human nature is the craving to be appreciated.
WILLIAM JAMES

Let There Be a *Shift*

The secret to rapid and astonishing success in fundraising seems to require a shift. Not a shift in what you are *doing* (although that will happen) but more of a shift in who you are *being*.

Most people trying to raise money are being *takers of money*. In their attitude and spirit and demeanor, they are taking something from someone else. They may be taking for a good cause or a good reason, but they are still taking.

But there is an inherent problem with being a taker. It does not feel powerful. It does not make one feel creative and full of fun with fresh ideas for raising money. If you are a taker, you are not at your best. Your self-esteem is not on the rise. You feel completely beholden to others, and you are almost always dealing with them from a weak position, a position of fear and anxiety. Why? Because being a taker does that to a person.

If you want to have great success in fundraising, you need to shift your thinking away from a self-concept of obsequious begging. You need to stand tall and proud when looking in the eyes of your donor. Because when you shift your thinking, you shift your whole way of being. You become someone who attracts money, not someone who makes it stay away.

If you are not raising the amount of money you would like to be raising, you need to create a major shift in your whole life's context: from being a taker to being a giver. In this book, you'll see with your own eyes that the act of giving works. You'll see that this fundamental shift in who you are being is a shift that will have enormous impact on every single fundraising conversation you have in the future.

Once you've got that fundamental shift going on in your life, you'll begin to see that there are many old fundraising myths that keep good organizations from raising money.

These myths have been built up over the years and may still stand like old condemned buildings blocking your view of the new horizon. Once you've shifted from taking to giving, the myths serve no function.

In the past, if you were a *taker,* the only function they served was to explain poor productivity. Notice that the myths are almost all about limitations to your ability to raise money. That's no accident. They serve a psychological purpose—that is, until you become a giver. Once you're a giver, the myths serve no more purpose.

Then they'll just get in the way.

These myths need to be exploded for us to truly begin anew. Otherwise, our organization will always be in a financial crisis. And, because of that underlying sense of crisis, we will never know how to fall in love with our work of raising money for a good cause.

This book will take those myths down.

EARTHQUAKE!

Have you ever seen news footage of buildings exploding during an earthquake? Earthquakes, triggered by a shift along fault lines in the earth, can cause entire city blocks of buildings to collapse into showers of debris.

Your own organization may need that big a shift. Right along your own fault lines. You will call it a *relation-shift,* because it alters forever the way you relate to the people you raise money from.

Relation*Shift*

FUNDRAISING'S 20 MOST DAMAGING MYTHS

MYTH #1

You Are Robin Hood

MYTH: *You as a fundraiser are in the business of* ***taking*** *money in order to give it to a good cause.*

REALITY SHIFT: *You as a fundraiser will now be* ***giving*** *instead of taking for a living.*

TAKE FROM THE RICH, GIVE TO THE POOR

The most dangerous fundraising myth of all is this: that you should take from the rich and give to the poor. If you see yourself in this Robin Hood role, you are not alone. Most people in fundraising do.

The problem with the Robin Hood concept is that it does not allow you to relax into free and productive relationships. As long as you think of yourself as a taker (even a good taker like Robin), you will be unable to expand your relationships with your donors. Because the more you take from them, the harder it will be to become close. And in the relation-shift paradigm, becoming close is vital.

Again, it is exactly this self-image of being a *taker* that destroys the effectiveness of a fundraiser (or anyone in any kind of relationship!). "Taking people's money" is what stops us from being able to receive a lot of money from people. But you can change that forever once you are willing to shift your mission from solicitation to *contribution*.

DID YOU SAY I HAD A LOT TO GIVE?

And you begin the process by realizing how much you have to contribute.

It's much more than you ever realized. For example, you have interesting *inside information* about your organization's good work to give. (Donors love inside news, gossip, information, predictions, etc.). You have *insight* to give. You have *access to important people* to give. You have *opportunities* to give. You have *accountability for success* to give.

And you have the most powerful gift of all: *acknowledgment*. The innovative, highly personalized thank-you. The unique and unforgettable communication of gratitude.

With all that to give your donors, there is no reason you can't stay focused on *giving* for the rest of your fundraising life. By doing this, you will always be comfortable with your donors. You will always be at ease. In fact, your relationship will feel very pleasantly reversed: When donors come up to you at a meeting or a social gathering, *they* will thank *you* when they see you. (That's when you know the shift has occurred, when your donor spots you across a crowded room, seems to brighten up, moves toward you, and begins the conversation with, "Hey, I just wanted to thank you!")

Relation-shifting from "taker" to "giver" will change totally and forever the way you see yourself and the way you feel about what you do.

YOU CAN'T HURRY LOVE

Fundraising is often likened to farming, especially with the use of such terms as "donor cultivation." Unfortunately, most charitable organizations leave themselves in the financial position of planting the seed today that they'll try to harvest tomorrow. They are like frantic farmers screaming at the damp ground, "Grow, you idiot, grow! I can't wait for the harvest time!"

In this instance, the weeding, fertilizing, watering, and nurturing of donors has been left out of the process. And because it has, no crops will grow. Because you can't hurry love.

You can't be desperate, on the one hand, and also raise substantial, long-term money. In fact, the more desperate you are, the less chance you have of succeeding. (This echoes the biblical saying, "To him that has more shall be given, from him that has not, it shall be taken away.")

Does this mean that in tough times you will never be able to communicate your most immediate need?

No. But it does mean that the only people who will be receptive to those urgent needs and willing to help you are going to be people with whom you have developed long, strong, trusting relationships. (This is especially true when the economy is down, and the only sure investment is the investment that is made in lifelong relationships.)

Charitable organizations must invest in their
relationships every day for those relationships
to be there in tough times.

KING HARVEST WILL SURELY NOT COME

This is where the farming analogy is most appropriate: it is not a matter of *hope* on the farmer's part that all of his sweat, toil and time will someday result in bountiful crops. It is a matter of knowing.

You, too, must produce the *certainty* of a great result by putting in the time. You must invest some energy. If you don't water your seedlings, there will be no harvest.

In fundraising you water the seedlings through service to the donor. Yes, that's a shift! The donor is not serving you as much as you are serving the donor. Instead of thinking that the only service is that provided by the donor's money, you must now shift to *providing him a service*. (Whenever we say "he" or "him" we also mean "she" or "her." We mean no offense to either gender, and we realize that women and men are equally qualified to be great donors.)

By providing your donor with inside information about your organization and innovative (and memorable!) acknowledgments of the difference he has made, you are building a relationship that will fund your future farther than the eye can see.

"It is a part of the great cosmic plan," wrote Napoleon Hill, "that no useful service shall be rendered by anyone without a just compensation."

BUT OH, THAT MAGIC FEELING

If someone were to ask you to recall the feeling you had when you performed your first charitable act in life, what would you recall?

Perhaps it was a time when you helped an elderly woman unload her groceries. Maybe you and your family once dropped off a load of clothing to the Goodwill center. Maybe you brought a needy family a Thanksgiving dinner.

Whatever your first charitable act was, you'll never forget that feeling . . . that very magical moment when you knew deep inside that you had enhanced the life of another human being. You had made a difference. Because you were here on earth, something was changed for the better.

It's what we all long for in the secret of our innermost being: the magic feeling of having made a difference.

Most charitable organizations have underestimated the power of that magic feeling. The awareness of that power gets lost in the distractions of the fundraising campaign, the annual appeal or the giving program. Instead of seeing his contribution as truly enhancing someone else's life, your donor can only see the tiny fleck of red his gift has made in the campaign thermometer (which is posted so prominently!).

And it is right there, in that well-intentioned thermometer, that the road to hell is embarked upon. Because that thermometer, and the absolutely impersonal campaign it symbolizes, cuts your donor off from his most important source of magic: the person being helped by his gift; the difference that was made.

Not to mention how small it makes your donor feel. When he sees a huge thermometer not nearly reaching its huge goal, his own gift looks even smaller than it is.

The result? There is no magic feeling at all. There is only another letter to the donor a year later asking for more money! How offensive that is: We are going to reward your giving by further attempts at taking.

The solution is to connect your donors to the people they are helping. Forget the thermometer, and forget the request for more money.

Put your donor in touch with the results of his giving. Let your donor experience *having made a difference in someone's life.*

Let your donor experience having been a contribution to the life of another. You will be thrilled at what happens after that.

WAS MY PUPPY PUT TO SLEEP?

Michael Bassoff tells this story:

First of all, you have to know this about me: I am a real sucker for animals. I love dogs. A couple of years ago I got one of those appeals from the Humane Society asking for money. On the outside of the envelope was a black-and-white photograph of an obviously malnourished puppy. It ripped my heart out!

I opened the letter and learned about Spot and all the other animals around the area that have been abused and need good homes. I was sold, so I sent a small contribution in the envelope provided.

Two weeks later I got a thank-you note. It was one of those form letters where a volunteer or staff person fills in the donor's name and the amount of the gift and then writes "thank you" at the bottom.

That was it. That was the end of my relationship.

A year later another Humane Society mailing arrived at my home. It was very similar to the first, but with a different dog on the envelope. Immediately my mind filled up with questions: What happened to the first dog?! Did the dog die? Was the dog adopted? Did it have puppies? Was it gassed?

They never told me what happened to that dog. And I know they're never going to tell me what happens to this year's dog. And that's exactly what's missing from this relationship: the magic feeling of seeing that dog given to a loving home. That magic feeling of knowing that my dollars made a difference.

Because without that feeling, without that relationship, why should I ever give again? In fact, not only do I not want to give again, I actually feel bitter!

My thinking goes this way: *These people only come around once a year when they need money! They don't give me any news of the countless hundreds of dogs that they might have saved and found homes for. I'm given no measurement of the suffering that they may have prevented by their good work. And I'm given no measure of the suffering I may have prevented.*

These are undoubtedly good people doing a wonderful service for society, but are they so worried about "fundraising" that they forgot why I might have given that money in the first place?

They neglected to do the things I needed most when I gave that contribution:

➤ Tell me what you did with the money.

➤ Tell me how I have enhanced a life.

➤ Tell me how I have made a difference. *And tell me at a time when you are not asking for more money!*

AND THEY CALL IT PUPPY LOVE

The humane society in this particular instance failed to make the fundamental shift: from *taking* from the donor to *giving* to the donor. Without that shift, no relationship can occur. A major gift is not even a consideration.

Their communications showed no understanding of how to create relationships.

When your organization solicits past donors without having demonstrated the *difference* their previous gifts made, the response will be minimal.

How might the humane society have avoided angering its donor? How might the donor have been "positioned" so that he would have wanted to make another donation?

Try to imagine what would have happened if a member of the society had turned up at our donor's door with a cute little dog. Just to show how that contribution had made a difference in Spot's life. What if the society representative then pulled out a series of snapshots showing a family with another newly adopted dog?

You might say, "Well who has time to drive all around town with a dog in the car?" Fair enough, then, what *do* we have time for? We'll certainly find time to draft and create another direct-mail piece and another solicitation. We might even find time for a special event (that most time-consuming of all activities) that barely breaks even. And we'll doubtless find time for long, frustrating meetings with our board members to discuss that latest financial crisis.

But if we drove the dog around, we would have no crisis to meet about. Our donors would take care of us in ways we can't even calculate. The truth is, we *do* have the time to do this. We just have to shift our thinking about what's the most important way to use our time.

House calls and snapshots are *exactly* what you need to be doing to build relationships. That's how small donors grow into major-gift–givers: through the careful and thoughtful building of relationships. And notice the key element in this story: it's not just empty attention, or fulsome thank-yous that this donor needs. It's information! He needed a vivid illustration of what his contribution did. He needed dramatic and informative thanking, not just thanking.

THANKS ARE NOT ENOUGH

If you are raising money for your organization, you have to be prepared to prove to your past donor that you have delivered what you said you would deliver. You and your board have to stay focused on that one mission: to find the most effective, novel and informative ways to be accountable to your donors. A thank-you note is not enough.

When a donor makes a contribution, it is because you have convinced him of something significant. You have convinced him that your organization's work is worthy and that his gift will make a difference.

You build your relationship with him by delivering evidence of the difference he has made. And you do it time and time again. You build your relationship by bringing your donor *into contact with the results of his donation.*

The example of bringing a dog to a person's home may seem like an exaggeration, but certainly showing the snapshots is not. You do the most you can. You go the extra mile. You make your donor feel very special. You make that donor feel appreciated.

Your donors are not looking for plaques, trophies, paperweights, address labels, bookends, commemorative pen sets, coffee cups, lapel pins, wall clocks, or testimonial dinners. They are giving you money so that you can provide a service to them—whether they realize that or not. You are providing the greatest service a human being can provide: evidence that they have *made a difference in the world.*

LET THEM BECOME INSIDERS

Here is another well-kept secret: Your donor longs to hear about the inside of your organization. Your donor longs for details about the service his donation has funded. He wants to be a spy in your organization's inner sanctum.

James Gregory Lord has written, "The more a donor feels like an insider, the greater stake he has in the success of the institution, and the larger an investment he can justify." Large investments are what solve all your financial problems!

Why not become masterful at attracting them? All you need to do is shift to giving your donor inside information and an insider's experience of your organization. You yourself are already on the inside, so you are not as excited by the magic of it as an outsider is. Maybe you were during the first few weeks you worked there. Remember that feeling? Get that feeling back into your imagination, and then give it to your donor. You need to remind yourself constantly that building relationships is what creates large investments, *nothing else.*

"There is a wonderful, mythical law of nature," wrote Peyton Conway March, "that the three things we crave most in life—happiness, freedom, and peace of mind—are always attained by giving them to someone else."

Once your relationship with your donor shifts from *taking-from-*the-donor to *giving-to*-the-donor, you will almost immediately set a metaphysical force into motion.

Once your donor communications shift from empty, depersonalized thank-yous to proof of difference-making, your major gifts will increase by a factor that will amaze you.

FUNDAMENTAL MYTH-BUSTING

The fundamental myth to be busted is the myth that you are Robin Hood, taking from the rich and giving to the poor.

In your new fundraising system, your reality shifts to this: You are giving thanks to the donor, giving to your organization, and giving the dramatic results of the whole process *back* to your donor. This completes the relation-shift cycle and inspires the perpetual giving of major gifts to your organization.

In life, the only meaning something has is the difference it makes. If it makes no difference, it has no meaning. Nothing short of the donor's whole life's meaning is at stake here! No matter who the person is, he has a life that can be meaningful, or not. As givers, we can be the agents of that meaningfulness. The bigger the sense of difference our donor gets, the bigger the future gets for our cause.

MYTH #2

Fundraising Is a Science

MYTH: *Fundraising is a science, and major gifts come from distinctive stages of manipulation:*
1. *Identification*
2. *Cultivation*
3. *Solicitation*

REALITY SHIFT: *Fundraising is a lost art—the art of relationship-building.*

FUNDRAISING AS WEIRD SCIENCE

The embarrassment we all feel at the thought of asking for money leads us to do many crazy things. One of the craziest (because it has become so institutionalized) has been to try to turn fundraising into an exact science.

All these attempts to remove creativity and human emotion from fundraising have led to such awkward absurdities as the famous Three Stages of Solicitation myth just mentioned.

There are variations on this myth, such as the Five I's (Identify, Interest, Intervene, Involve and Invest). And all are an attempt to establish a scientific procedure in place of the relationship art that fundraising really is.

And the truth is that relationships don't work in scientific stages. Sometimes you'll meet a person and in fifteen minutes you are talking to her as if you've known her for years. When you really hit it off with someone, you immediately have a relationship that is so powerful, *anything* can come out of it.

We can't possibly reduce anything as powerful as a relationship between two human beings down to identification, cultivation and solicitation. It's too human and organic for that; like an organism, the relationship suffers when you try to cut it into parts.

If you are consoling somebody who has just lost a spouse to heart disease and helping her to establish a memorial fund, it can be a very emotional and rapid act. Would you interrupt the act to separate the "cultivation" from the "solicitation"? We think not.

If you have to examine a relationship to see what stage of cultivation or solicitation it is in, the chances are that your relationship is so artificial you won't raise any money from it anyway.

The only way to have a friend is to be one.
RALPH WALDO EMERSON

YOU'VE GOT A FRIEND

One way to understand good fundraising relationships is to compare them to the relationships you've created in your own personal life. Did you scientifically identify, cultivate, and then solicit your best friend to become your best friend? Did you follow a step-by-step process to assure a successful "ask"?

Great relationships in fundraising happen the same way great friendships happen. You get to know people, you share things with them, and you are intrigued by them. You become part of their lives and they become part of your life.

You need a fundraising relationship in which—as in a friendship—anything can happen and anything can be discussed. This is especially true in the area of planned giving. The greatest barrier to arranging planned gifts to your organization is fear . . . fear of talking to people about their wills and trusts.

And of course you can't talk to people you barely know about their wills and trusts. But you can certainly talk to friends.

If your relationship with a potential donor seems to be stuck on hold, ask yourself what you would do if this were a close friend of yours. If you are fearful about taking the donor's time for a presentation, then don't do the presentation. Create a relationship. Large gifts come from relationships, not presentations. Instead, go see him to thank him personally for his interest, then simply find out more about his life and his interests. Don't have an agenda. When you meet with your best friend, do you bring an agenda?

HOW TO BE A CLOWN FISH

Some of our fundraising seminars prior to *RelationShift* carried the title: *The Symbiosis System*. We'd open our talks with a discussion of the clown fish and the sea anemone, and how badly they needed each other for survival.

We would try to dramatize the interdependence of nature's creatures and vegetation under the sea, and draw the parallel between those symbiotic relationships and the relationship you need to have with your donor.

We also used another metaphor to illustrate the benefits of giving to a donor rather than taking. We talked about the old gold miner's scale, and we urged our clients to always add nuggets of gold to the donor's side of the scale so that the "balance of debt" would be in your organization's favor.

We wanted our clients' donors always to be saying, "I don't know why they're going to all that trouble for me when, after all, I only gave them_____ (fill in the blank)."

Keep tipping the balance. What can you give today? Something small. Something large. Keep adding nuggets so that the balance of perceived indebtedness is always building in your favor. You want a major group of major donors who always feel grateful when they think of your name. That's the shift!

THE UNGRATEFUL DONOR

Your personal transformation from an arm-twister to a relationship-builder should become comprehensive. There should be no sense of being a giver one minute and a taker the next, even if you encounter the occasional ungrateful donor.

The service you provide (delivering information, dramatic proof of results, and thoughtful thank-yous) should always continue. Don't be disappointed if your ungrateful donor doesn't seem to appreciate your efforts right away. The results of seed-sowing take time.

Take the case of Laird Fletcher, for example. (Not his real name. In fact all donor names and identities in this book have been altered to protect their privacy.) Laird Fletcher, to put it simply, was not a very pleasant man. His smallish gifts to our organization always seemed to be accompanied by a laconic remark.

"You've got a lot of well-dressed people raising money for your organizations," Laird Fletcher would say. "What percent of the dollars you raise goes to a clothing allowance?"

Despite his irritating behavior, Mr. Fletcher somehow attracted the concern of one of our administrative assistants.

"For some reason," Jennifer would say, "I like this man. Maybe he just reminds me of my father, who on the surface tried to be the crankiest man who ever lived."

Jennifer began to counter Laird Fletcher's grouchy remarks with a pleasant smile and an expression of gratitude. With our active encouragement, Jennifer decided to make our organization's relationship with Mr. Fletcher her own private project.

She took to the challenge with great enthusiasm. She indulged her fondness for gift and card shops and began sending Fletcher cute cards with long handwritten notes. The notes updated him on our organization's real use of his donation money ("No, there's no clothing allowance, sir") and always ended with a personal note of thanks.

She made a point of remembering his birthday (although he protested with a wry remark about buttering him up "for a bigger gift"). And she also began writing him to celebrate the anniversary of his first small gift to the organization. (This gift anniversary innovation by Jennifer has since been used elsewhere with great success!)

And through the years Mr. Fletcher's gifts remained very small, but they were consistent.

Finally one day the news arrived that Laird Fletcher had died in his sleep. And despite his advanced years and mercifully peaceful passing, Jennifer was deeply saddened. At the invitation of Fletcher's widow, she attended the funeral.

"You meant more to him than he wanted anyone to know," his widow told Jennifer at a private gathering after the services. "He saved all your cards, and I know he read them often. Every report you sent him about your organization was also saved and filed carefully. You made an impact. And I think you'll be pleased to know that he's left something for your organization in his will."

Jennifer was quite moved. She thanked Mrs. Fletcher and returned to her job the following Monday without giving the matter another thought. Two months later a phone call came from Mrs. Fletcher's lawyer, requesting a meeting with Jennifer, her organization's lawyer, and the director.

At that meeting the lawyer and Mrs. Fletcher presented the organization with a donation that exceeded half a million dollars, "to be donated in the memory of Mr. Laird Fletcher."

THREE TOUGH LESSONS

The story of Laird Fletcher provided us with three lessons (and they're lessons that are sometimes difficult to remember):

Lesson Number One: When you are targeting your communications to various groups of prospects, publics, and even donors, don't overlook the power of the most important communication of all: one-on-one communication. Even one-on-one communication with "ungrateful donors" of "small gifts" can produce astonishing results.

If you serve an ungrateful master, serve him the more.
Put God in your debt. Every stroke shall be repaid.
The longer the payment is withheld, the better for you;
for compound interest on compound interest is the rate
and usage of this exchequer.
RALPH WALDO EMERSON

Lesson Number Two: Involve everyone, even the temps and assistants, in the job of thanking donors and building relationships with them. Some of your biggest gifts will come from donors who built relationships with the most unlikely people.

Lesson Number Three: Never underestimate the power of a handwritten card or letter. Letter-writing is rapidly becoming a lost art in this age of high-tech audio and electronic communications. Don't let it become a lost art in your organization. Most of your best donors grew up writing and receiving good letters, and they miss the experience. Many of your best donors are over sixty years old and are not as comfortable with electronic communication as younger people are. They appreciate good letters more than you might realize.

HOW TO WRITE A GREAT LETTER

There is no step-by-step guide that supersedes the primary suggestion of writing *from the heart.*

Once you make sure you've done that, the best guidelines are these:
➤ Does your letter connect your donor to the good his gift has done?
➤ Is it an inspired message?

What's an inspired message? You'll know it when you see it. It goes beyond the expected. It is touching and vulnerable. It sometimes causes a little chill or even a tear when you read it.

How do you do it? Write what would move *you.* Write the note that you would like to get. Take your time. Don't send it until you know it connects. (Red Smith's remark about how to create inspired writing comes to mind: "It's easy," he said. "You just open a vein and begin.")

One of the advantages of heartfelt one-on-one correspondence is that it doesn't have to survive review by committee. Most nonprofit newsletters, mass mailings, press releases, and communications to groups of any kind lack feeling. They are written more to avoid disapproval than they are to really touch someone.

Therefore, most mass communications from your organization have two strikes against them to begin with:
➤ They are not personal, and can make no friendly reference to the individual recipient.

➤ They are too safe and sterile to convey the real excitement of your cause. (Most direct mail is extremely boring. Not that it matters—it doesn't get read anyway.)

Communications with individual donors are more important than your mass communications. Not only can you improve a relationship more dramatically in an individual communication, but your communication will be going directly to the source of more than eighty percent of all charitable donations: the individual donor!

MYTH #3

Planned Gifts Depend On Death

MYTH: *Your planned gifts have no value until your donor passes away.*

REALITY SHIFT: *Living donors of planned gifts are money in the bank. The security you build for your organization through planned gifts can and should be best appreciated **while the donor is alive**.*

LIVING, BREATHING ENDOWMENTS

Most administrators dream of endowments. Most would like to have enough of an endowment to survive on the interest earned by that endowment forever! No more headaches ever again. A guaranteed future.

But isn't that what planned gifts do for you? Planned gifts are your endowment and your future.

When people say that upon their death, or upon the death of their spouse, your institution will get a certain amount of money, what they're really doing is ensuring your future. And the younger that person is, the further off into the future you are insured.

But you might say, "We need money right *now!*"

The secret is this: When you shift from money-solicitation to relationship-building, you will have so many of these relationships, so many donors who consider your institution a *loved one,* that all periods of future time are insured.

You *want* your donors to live long lives. They are family. The longer they live, the better. The longer they live, the more they talk about you to *their* friends and family. The more they talk, the more relationships appear at your doorstep. And the longer your planned givers live, the further your institution's financial security stretches into the future.

AMERICA GROWS OLDER

Each year there are more and more healthy, bright and active senior citizens. There are now more than 40 million people over the age of 65 in the United States!

And if you had to guess what magazine had the largest circulation in the United States, would you believe that it was *Modern Maturity,* with over 22 million readers?!

This graying of the population is an enormous benefit to fundraisers. There are simply more people than ever positioned to help you. Are you positioned to help them?

Adweek's Marketing Week summed it up this way, "An era dominated by youth is ending. What we eat; what we wear; where, how and when we travel; what we buy and why we buy it—all will change as vast numbers of consumers face opportunities and milestones of their journey beyond youth."

The word "consumers" here need not be changed to "donors." Let's leave it as "consumers," because there is an important insight into relation-shifting here that should not be lost.

Donors *are* consumers. The moment you fully accept that truth, and make it a part of all your operating strategies, is the moment of great abundance flowing into your organization.

Older donors "consume" information about their good works, and they "consume" innovative thank-yous from you.

So, do you now simply begin to focus on customer satisfaction? Not really, because satisfaction is not enough! You might want to strive for something called *customer delight*.

Customer satisfaction is completely neutral. It really means "no bad word-of-mouth." If you have a satisfying experience at a retail store, a repair garage, or a bank, are you going to tell your friends and loved ones about it? No. You are satisfied and you expect to be satisfied.

To get good word-of-mouth generated, you need to create *customer delight*. Delighted people talk. People who are pleasantly surprised talk. And when older Americans talk to each other, they trust each other, and soon you find that your planned givers are multiplying.

MYTH #4

A Down Economy Is Bad for Fundraising

MYTH: *It is more difficult to raise money in a down economy.*

REALITY SHIFT: *The statistics dramatically demonstrate that a down economy has no substantial effect on charitable giving, and while others are wringing their hands over the imaginary gloom, you can build stronger relationships than ever before.*

SELF-FULFILLING PROPHECIES

Because so many people in the nonprofit field *believe* that it's harder to raise money in a down economy, there is actually *more* money available to you when the economy turns down, because fewer people are pressing positively to raise it.

Our life is what our thoughts make it.
MARCUS AURELIUS ANTONIUS

In times of economic stagnation, board members have seemed to fasten on the "down economy" or the "recession" as the most fashionable excuse for not raising money.

"The banks are going out of business, or are being bought by larger banks from out of state," they lament. "Our local builders and developers, on whom we used to rely so heavily, are having a hard time even staying in business."

The complaints go on and on.

But the truth is that none of that matters. This is just the latest fad in excuses. The truth is that a downturned economy will only affect the most inefficient and unprofitable methods of raising money.

The real money (where more than eighty percent of all charitable giving comes from) not only remains unaffected by a down economy, but actually becomes a bigger and better opportunity for you. That's because the real money (eighty percent of all money raised!) comes from individual donors.

Certainly people are more particular about where they put their money in a down economy. But that favors you. Because they are more circumspect about spending it and wasting it, they actually have more available for a good cause.

Also, because you have shifted your philosophy to relationship-building, the gifts of accountability you give are just what the particular donor craves. You account for what the donor's money does, down to the most personal detail. Your standard is for an unreasonably thorough accountability. Careful donors love that, and tend to move money *away* from nonaccountable charities over to yours.

Another plus for you in a down economy is that financially secure donors are more aware that times are now difficult for insecure sources of money. Strong donors feel their importance even more.

Finally, a down economy is just a circumstance, and circumstances are *not* the focus of great fundraisers. Relationships are.

A down economy is one of many circumstances used by some fundraisers to explain a poor performance. This tendency continually to point to circumstances usually comes from a sense of powerlessness. As long as they are operating out of a self-image of "taker," they will not feel the inner personal power necessary to create success.

But the good news is that the reverse is also true. Once they commit completely to relationship-building as their fundraising method, their power increases ten times over that of their former taker-selves—because they are now doing something different for a living. Instead of being a walking, talking solicitation, they are being an ongoing, living contribution. Their whole *life* becomes a series of giving acts. Self-esteem soars. A sense of personal power increases, and the power of circumstance is reduced to almost nothing. We have seen this transformation time and time again, and we have seen it yield millions of unexpected dollars.

DOWN SO LONG IT LOOKS LIKE UP

Statistics show that over the past ten years, charitable giving has continued to grow at enormous rates—rates unaffected by the economy.

The down economy will have no more adverse effect on your team's success than it would have on the success of the Washington Redskins.

"Our only limitations," said Napoleon Hill, "are the ones we set up in our minds."

People are always blaming their circumstances for what they are. I don't believe in circumstances. The people who get on in this world are the people who get up and look for the circumstances they want, and if they can't find them they make them.
GEORGE BERNARD SHAW

Finally, your best donors are largely unaffected by the swings in the economy. They are not as actively engaged in the economy because their money has already been made. It is being held high above the choppy waters of day-to-day commerce. (It is being held up there for you.)

Older Americans, those already in retirement (there are more than 60 million of them—and their percentage of the population is growing every year!) are only marginally affected by any current economic ebb or flow.

One of the gravest mistakes nonprofit organizations make is spending a disproportionate amount of their time courting the younger movers and shakers in their communities. What they don't understand is that they are courting people who are more likely to panic when the economy goes bump in the night. And because these younger people are more jittery, they offer a much less stable basis for major-gift fundraising.

This is when a kind of *court shift* is badly needed! You need to lower the percentage of time you spend courting yuppies and highly visible young community luminaries, and increase the time you spend courting old Aunt Tilly, who also longs to help you out.

The economy will continue to be volatile in years to come. That will work in your favor if you use down times to build relationships in an even stronger way. The only sure investment in these economic times is your investment in a relationship.

The same is true for changes in the tax code. When estate tax laws change and people have more money available, they will give it to their best relationships.

When the down economy finally swings upward and more wealth is created, that wealth will go to *the relationships created when the economy was down.*

It's All in Who You Know

MYTH: *It's all in who you know.*

REALITY SHIFT: *It's actually **how well** you know them. Your "contacts" with the rich and famous are meaningless compared to your long-term, carefully built relationships.*

IT'S NOT A CONTACT SPORT

Many fundraising meetings focus on "contacts." Board members and staff sit around over coffee and ask: Who's our contact at the bank? Who's our contact in the mining industry? Who's our contact in the insurance industry? Who are the big names? How can we get to the community leaders and decision-makers?

In reality, those contacts are often far too superficial to make a real difference. Because unless those contacts are also long-term committed relationships, they are not going to really help you. They're not going to give you *their* contacts, nor are they going to go out and solicit major gifts for your cause.

Contacts are valuable only if they are in the process of being converted to staunch supporters of the cause. When they are merely contacts, they create the illusion of value without really having any.

Keep this in mind at all times: relationships *generate money, contacts don't. Contacts merely generate the illusion of influence. Focus on developing relationships.*

Think about the whole "contact" concept: For example, would it be possible that you could be planning on marrying your contact at the bank? He or she certainly wouldn't be just a contact any more at that stage!

It's helpful to think of your mission as related to a lifetime commitment, not totally unlike a marriage. After all, you are talking about asking people to give you their lifelong earnings and savings! To just give it to you! Wow. No wonder people are afraid. No wonder people see themselves as takers and shrink all day from real fundraising and hide behind meaningless activity.

You're basically asking people to give you a part of everything they have worked for in a lifetime. Are they going to give that to a mere contact? Would you?

Contacts don't raise money. Relationships do.

A contact is a seed, but a relationship is a bountiful tree. One fruitful relationship with one major individual donor will yield your organization more money than a hundred casual contacts.

You've Got To Get
The Word Out

MYTH: *We've got to get the word out (because nobody out there knows about us!).*

REALITY SHIFT: *"Getting the word out" to the masses is absolutely unimportant compared to keeping your individual donors well informed.*

THE AGE OF THE INDIVIDUAL

Because the average consumer hears and sees over five hundred advertising and sales messages a day, most mass marketing has become little more than clutter.

Nonprofits need to catch on to the secret that entrepreneurial business marketers have discovered: You need to communicate with individuals, not masses. It's the only thing that works.

The authors of the best-selling *Megatrends* books of forecasts, John Naisbitt and Patricia Aburdene, summarize their statistical findings this way: "Recognition of the individual is the thread connecting every future trend we see."

In *The Great Marketing Turnaround*, marketing gurus Stan Rapp and Tom Collins write, "In this new age the smartest advertisers will establish direct contact with the consumer, whether before or after the first sale, and use that contact to gain customer loyalty and market share by building a mutually rewarding relationship."

Most business marketers have learned the expensive folly of "getting the word out" into the cluttered marketplace. Many now-defunct dotcom companies rose quickly and flared out after overspending on massive TV campaigns. We remember their names, like Pets.com, because they truly got the word out. But they are gone, because they didn't create relationships with customers.

Getting the word out to the general public is the most overrated and futile endeavor taken on by nonprofits everywhere. It is a misguided superstition that wastes time and money. Yet nonprofit board members will often hesitate to become enthusiastic about raising money for you until they know a lot of public relations work has taken place.

"We can't just go out and ask people for money!" they will cry. "We've got to get the word out first!"

The only word you have to worry about getting out is the highly specialized word-of-mouth. And that word-of-mouth happens when one of your happy relationships talks to friends, associates and relatives about your organization.

YOU DON'T HAVE TO SET
THE WORLD ON FIRE

Just start a little flame in one donor's heart. Just create one great relationship with one donor.

The Scripps Institute in San Diego, internationally recognized for its tremendous success at raising money, raises more than ninety-five percent of its money from twenty-seven individual donors.

That's correct: twenty-seven donors!

Try this exercise: Pretend that all the contributions you need in the future can only come from twenty-seven donors each year. Then choose, from among your current donor list, who those twenty-seven donors will be. Pick the twenty-seven people who are most involved and most committed to your organization.

Then make a list of the ten things you are going you do with each one of these twenty-seven donors to strengthen your relationship with them over the next two months.

➤ What are the ways in which you can bring them into your organization?

➤ How can you better inform them about the services you are providing and the people whose lives you are touching?

➤ How can you introduce them to the people who have been touched by your organization?

➤ How can you put a very human face on the difference their money has made?

➤ How can you thank them?

➤ How can you get other people to thank them?

(And if you are in an arts organization, do not for a minute think that you do not touch lives. You do—sometimes in ways that are deeper and even more personal than the ways of medical or more conventionally altruistic organizations.)

Remember, the huge amounts of money raised by the Scripps Institute should send a signal to all nonprofit organizations.

After you've really thought about the money you could raise from just twenty-seven donors, then you're ready for an even more advanced exercise. Try this: imagine that you are restricted to raising all your money from a *single* donor. That's right, just one.

Too absurd?

Not so fast. There are now more than a million millionaires in the United States. And there are over one hundred billionaires!

We've had people leave the organizations to which we've taught relation-shifting half of all they had. If a billionaire left you half his assets, could you survive for a while on five hundred million dollars?

Pick that one donor of yours who is committed enough to leave you the most (notice we did not say "rich enough," because the commitment is more important). Then start building your relationship with him or her. What would you do?

When you've fantasized about how you would treat that person and what you would to bring him or her deeper into the heart of your organization, you will begin to realize how all of your committed donors should be treated. And once they are treated that way, you will be pleasantly surprised at the increase in donations.

And, no, you won't have to *ask* for the money.

"The more a donor feels like an insider," says James Gregory Lord, "the greater stake he has in the success of the institution, and the larger investment he can justify."

Maybe it's time to stop worrying about getting the word out, and start concentrating on getting the word "in."

You can begin to make your communications an inside job, directed at the many great relationships you already have and making those relationships even more powerful.

FRUIT FROM THE SWEETHEART TREE

Concentrate on those few good people who have already given to your cause. Cut your focus down to the best donors you already have. Get to know them better. Show them the ways you make a difference in the world. Show them the ways they can make a difference. Involve them in a higher level in your organization. Help them learn more about what you are doing, and how they can help you do what you want to do. Prune down to the few, then take care of those few!

Prune your donor tree and watch it grow.

Ralph Waldo Emerson might as well have been talking about fundraising when he said, "As the gardener, by severe pruning, forces the sap tree into one or two vigorous limbs, so should you cut off your miscellaneous activity and concentrate your force on a few points."

THE CRUMPLED THERMOMETER

Once, during one of our development seminars, we passed out to our group a piece of paper with a handsome illustration on it of a fundraising campaign thermometer. Once our participants had the thermometer illustrations in their hands, we asked them to crumple them up and throw them into the center of the room.

We were trying to imprint a point: Your organization's fundraising goals should remain internal and not be what you focus your donor on. Otherwise the donor will see himself as a small speck of ink in that thermometer, instead of an enormous force in the success of your cause.

A goal is a great thing for you and your staff and even board members to have, because it's hard to hit a target if you don't know where it is. But your goal can become too prominent in the organization's consciousness. Soon false science takes over, and the quantified goal replaces the very human donor in your people's thoughts.

Just as plays in the huddle are not broadcast to the crowd, neither should your goals for raising money be the public focus of what you are about. That's just more false science where the art of relationship-building should be.

And there *are* good ways to mass-distribute your information—but that's not what this book is about. This book is about shifting away from the mass approach.

Most nonprofits spend far too much time working on "getting the word out" to large groups. Too much time is spent on newsletters, press releases, public service announcements, mass mailings, special-event publicity, and on and on.

Too much time, money, and effort are being directed at communicating to groups of people instead of communicating to individual people.

Remember that the individual donor gives more than eighty percent of the 100 million dollars raised for charity each year!

REVERSING CONVENTIONAL WISDOM

Most nonprofits focus their communication strategies on targets that are too large. They are lost because they're following the retail marketing strategies of the sixties, seventies and eighties.

Those strategies have been thoroughly and convincingly debunked by today's best and most perceptive marketing analysts, Stan Rapp and

Tom Collins. In their cutting-edge book, *The Great Marketing Turn-around,* Rapp and Collins describe why today's most dramatic market-ing successes are turning "away from the old ways of mass marketing and toward a new kind of individualized marketing." Today's compa-nies, say Rapp and Collins, "can succeed by making a single basic shift in thinking which is reversal of what was the conventional wisdom in the '60s, '70s and '80s."

That "single basic shift" has already been made by the world's most successful fundraisers. And it's the same shift, away from mass market-ing toward individualized marketing. Or: away from the massive cam-paign and toward the individual relationship.

Most progressive businesses today would envy you. As a fundraiser, you are in possession of a precious database: your lists of donors.

WATCH WHAT HAPPENS

When we are called in to improve the fundraising success of an organ-ization, we will often begin by running an experiment: We make a modest donation to the client organization under a name they do not recognize. Then we watch what happens. Learning firsthand how donors are thanked teaches us more about the problems in the organi-zation than almost anything else we could do.

Recently, we donated to a client we were working with. The organi-zation was a large zoo. Their donations had fallen off in recent years and they didn't know why.

We did receive a letter back thanking us for the donation, and ad-mittedly the letter was well written and signed by the director himself (although it was certainly in the computer as a form). Not surprisingly, the letter left out the most important part: What did you do with the money?

Now, of course, it's not always possible to tell a donor where his spe-cific hundred dollars is going to be applied. But you can come close enough. You can write enthusiastically about current projects being funded with current donation money (of which his gift is an important part).

As that zoo's donor, we would have loved to hear about the new habitat being built for the baby polar bear and the new zoologist being hired to work with the small animals in the zoo's new addition.

There is lots of fascinating information your donor longs to hear about—especially if you connect it to the gift that donor just gave.

And what about a handwritten P.S. from the person who is caring for the polar bears?

DONOR PHONERS

Talking to your donors by telephone falls somewhere between personal visits and great letters. Phone calls are often a vital component of relationship-building, but they can also be tricky.

Some of your older donors may not be comfortable communicating by phone. You know who they are, and you can often sense it when you call them. They have a strangely distant approach to a phone conversation—but then they talk to you warmly when you see them in person.

That's another reason why across-the-board thanking and acknowledgment systems fail—they don't take into account each donor's individual sensitivity.

FOOTBALL OVER THE PHONE

One of our clients was a major college football team that needed to improve season-ticket sales.

Like most sports teams who deal with season-ticket renewals, their communications were coldly bureaucratic. There was even a kind of IRS-like feeling to the notices: It's that time of the year. We expect you to give again. It's your duty.

Would people really like to give gifts to the IRS?

One good idea our client thought of to create the warmth necessary to good fundraising communications was the idea of the coach and player phone call. One of the hidden treasures many nonprofits have is the celebrity status of some of their members. Often an arts group or a political team fails to capitalize on that celebrity to thank donors in a powerful and memorable way.

For one full day, the coaches and star players sat in a large conference room, ate pizza, drank pop, and made phone calls to season-ticket buyers.

When the popular head coach of a major college football team you've watched for years calls you personally on the phone, you never forget it.

Ticket buyer: Hello?

Head coach: Hello, is this Robert Malmberg?

Ticket buyer: Yes.

Head coach: Robert, this is Coach Dick Armstrong calling, and I just wanted to thank you for buying your season tickets this year.

Ticket buyer: Wait a minute, are you kidding, is this really Dick Armstrong?

Head coach: It sure is, Robert. I just wanted you to realize how important you are to us this year. As you know, we have a tough home schedule—we play UCLA, Washington, and Oklahoma at home this year—and we need your kind of support to help get the guys motivated enough to take a real shot at those teams.

Ticket buyer: Well, I don't really know what to say. It's just really incredible that you're calling me. Wait until I tell my family.

Head coach: Well, thank you, Robert, for your support, and give my best to your family.

That phone call took less than a minute. But the long-term impression it made will last a lifetime.

The celebrity status of political figures is also often overlooked by their fundraisers. One of our clients was a popular United States congressman. We noticed that because his staff sat in long, boring meetings day after day with the congressman, they had lost sight of his status with contributors. It turned out that a day of phoned thank-yous from a United Sates congressman to his donors can go a long way to strengthening relationships.

Your own organization may have luminaries connected to it who could work wonders for you if you turned them loose on donors. We will often ask doctors associated with one of our organizations to call donors, or write to them directly, and explain how helpful their gifts have been and exactly what those gifts are now making possible. You may think that donors are not interested in the medical research eso-terica that our doctors ramble on about, but you would be wrong. They are absolutely fascinated!

Picking high-profile people in your organization to deliver thank-yous for you is one of the most powerful things you can do for your or-ganization. To you, those people have lost their celebrity status long ago. But to your donors, they have not.

ONLY THE SURPRISING SURVIVE

Despite our urging to not waste time on mass media, it is true that using a certain amount of it is inevitable. Therefore, for the absolutely necessary distribution of public relations information, we recommend the following rules:

1. Utilize the element of surprise.
Always look at your letters, newsletters, press releases, etc., before they go out and ask, "Is this going to surprise people?" Anything that does not capture the reading or viewing audience is going to fail to make an impression because of the sheer volume of messages people are exposed to each day. And yes, your information can be surprising if you look hard enough for your story and become creative about the presentation.

The element of surprise is important because it's the only approach we've found that does not permit boredom. Your communications should never be allowed to be boring. And nothing can be simultane-ously surprising and boring.

Have you ever written a fundraising letter and watched someone yawn while reading it? "A yawn," said G. K. Chesterton, "is a silent scream."

2. Always feature people.

In everything from your newsletter photos to your video footage to your direct-mail letter's stories, use real people being touched in real ways by your organization's work. The candid, unposed photo will attract twice the attention (and retention) that posed photos do. In press conferences or radio interviews, the unrehearsed talks from the heart will be more powerful than the carefully read document.

(And don't be afraid to use the advice of Winston Churchill, who said about public speaking, "If you have an important point to make, don't try to be subtle or clever. Use a pile driver. Hit the point once. Then come back and hit it again. Then hit a third time—a tremendous whack.")

Even in written communications, it is effective to feature interesting quotes from intriguing real people. The key element is *real people*. Because if you misdirect the heart of your communications to facts, figures, goals, buildings, projects, campaigns, and thermometers, you lose all of your communication's potential for fundraising.

In all your communications, remember to check to make sure they are featuring *people*. You will never think of anything more interesting to write about than people, so why waste precious time trying?

3. Relate to the media.

If a story is written about your organization, thank the writer and the photographer who worked on it. This seems elementary, but it is a rare practice! If a television station does a story, keep track of the names of everyone who worked with you and thank them individually in individual ways.

If a good job was done in reporting about your organization, never forget to praise the journalists involved and let them know exactly why you thought their work was good. Most people in the media voice a common complaint: their work goes unappreciated, and the moment it's run, it's yesterday's news. Praise them, and their relationship with you will grow.

There is an inherent law of mind that we increase whatever we praise. The whole of creation responds to praise, and is glad. Animal trainers pet and reward their charges with delicacies for acts of obedience; children glow with joy and gladness when they are praised. Even vegetation grows better for those who love it.
CHARLES FILLMORE

YOU ARE THE SUNSHINE

We've mentioned fundraising's affection for farming as a development metaphor. The trouble is, most fundraisers get hung up on the early stages, such as donor cultivation, and don't carry out the metaphor to its best application.

By shifting from mass marketing to relationship marketing, you will be planting the seeds of faith. You will be concentrating your most creative communication skill on single donors. Sometimes it will feel like a lost effort, because the creativity you pour into a single letter to a single donor might have been something you'd have liked to see go out en masse to a few thousand prospects.

But your faith will pay you with a rich harvest. Our clients have proven this time and time again. Keep sowing those seeds into the ground of relationship, and your donations will increase.

No ray of sunshine is ever lost, but the green which it awakens into existence needs time to grow; and it is not always granted to the sower to see the harvest. All the work that is worth anything is done in faith.
ALBERT SCHWEITZER

All the work you do that is worth anything is work that touches the heart of your donor. If your communications efforts can be shifted away from boring bureaucratic releases to fascinating and touching interpersonal communications, you will succeed beyond your wildest dreams.

MEMBERSHIPS OF GOLD

One of the biggest successes we ever had in fundraising was begun by a massive direct-mail campaign. The millions raised from this project are often talked about as a glowing example of what great direct mail can do.

But that kind of talk always misses the point. The success we had with the project came long *after* the direct-mail prospecting occurred.

One of our clients asked us what we would do to introduce their organization to a small but wealthy retirement community a few miles south of the big city. There was said to be half a billion dollars on deposit in that small community's few little banks, and our client's eyes grew large every time that fact was discussed.

We created a direct-mail package that offered a membership and a program of involvement with the organization for the donor. The cost of a lifetime membership was only $100, and what we offered in the way of special tours, private briefings by doctors, luncheons, white papers, etc. was quite disproportionate to the membership cost.

We did not ask for renewals, and we never appealed to members for more money. All we did was over-deliver on the hundred dollars. All we did was thank and thank and thank. We treated those original members like royalty. They got tours of the facilities, and we met with them regularly to have top research doctors speak about the latest in medical breakthroughs.

Those donors who had paid $100 for a lifetime membership were being treated by everyone in our organization as if they'd each given $10,000.

To some cynics observing what we were doing, this whole project seemed crazy and ill-advised. That was until the retirement community's unofficial "mayor," Wylie E. Seaholm, gave us an unexpected six-figure gift! Suddenly the project was being called "interesting" instead of "loony."

Soon more and more gifts of all sizes came in, and it wasn't long before many of the retirees were changing their will to include our organization—sometimes in very big ways.

Millions have come out of that initial mailing, but certainly not as a result of the mailing alone. The millions come in response to how the initial $100 donors were *treated*. And what we hear praised as a great "direct-mail success" was not a direct-mail success at all, but rather a relationship-building success.

However, that direct-mail package did have one important element that we should point out: It did not use a diversion to attract a small donation. It used the *appeal of the organization* and nothing else. Therefore, the donors who did respond were not responding to a bake sale, a 10k run, or a trip to London, but rather to our cause.

Never in the history of the world has there been such abundant opportunity as there is now for the person who is willing to serve before trying to collect.
NAPOLEON HILL

YOU CAN BE UNREASONABLE

Your projects that involve creative communications should never conform to what everyone else does. And every project you create that insists on serving before trying to collect will be opposed by the more reasonable members of your organization. The only way to convince them is to do what the Nike ads say: "Just do it."

In the movie *Little Man Tate*, one of the child geniuses quotes George Bernard Shaw to another child. He says, "The reasonable man adapts to the world around him. The unreasonable man tries to make the world adapt to him. Therefore all progress is made by the unreasonable man."

WHAT IS YOUR REAL APPEAL?

One problem nonprofits seem to have is in fully understanding their own real appeal. If you don't understand your real appeal, it is very difficult to produce a successful prospecting type of communication such as the direct-mail piece mentioned above.

"One of the most important things an organization can do," says management consultant Peter Drucker, "is determine exactly what kind of business it is in."

One of the best rules of thumb in locating your own real appeal is this: Ask other people. Don't trust yourself to know, because you may be too close to see it.

Talk to donors who have already given and find out what it is about your organization that attracted them. And by all means talk to the beneficiaries of your organization's good work. Let them tell you what your organization has done for them, and why it was important. In listening to others you will find your real appeal.

PULL YOUR ANCHOR AND SHIFT AWAY

Shift away from the bureaucratic and boring. Shift away! Shift toward relationships, even in your more formal communications. Yes, even in your newsletters, mass mailings, press releases, PSAs, and the rest. Shift toward people.

Before you send a mass communication out, study it. Does it have people in it? Are they real people caught in the act of being human, or are they posing and pontificating in a bureaucratic and boring way?

Your communications should tell stories. They should never feel like somebody "wrote" them.

Your own communications will be as powerful as the people they talk about.

Try to focus all your communications on people: people helped by your organization, people who help your organization, and people who do your organization's most intriguing work.

When you pick up a communication that does not obsessively focus on people, you will know that you have picked up a boring and bureaucratic communication.

SOME TURTLES ARE GOOD PEOPLE

It is important to know that you can sometimes enlarge the definition of "people" (especially if you are a zoo or an animal-rights group) to include "beings that are dear to us." Some pet owners say, "Pets are like people, only better."

The story of the emaciated little puppy in the beginning of this book makes the point abundantly clear.

A famous successful direct-mail fundraising piece by the Center for Environmental Education in Washington, D.C., featured pictures of baby turtles crawling down along the right-hand margin of the letter. The letter's first sentence was: "Will you take a moment to consider the desperate plight of the baby sea turtles to your right?"

THIS OLD MAN

The American birth rate is dropping and longevity is rising. Marketing analysts Rapp and Collins report that "the 'new old' are emerging—healthy, vigorous, and solvent. The 26% of the population over age 50 controls three-fourths of the nation's financial assets."

Because people over fifty years old control over three-fourths of the nation's assets, it would empower your organization to address its communications to that target audience. Making the proper shift in focus to people over fifty will yield tremendous results for you in the future.

One of the positive qualities most often found in older donors is their capacity for self-renewal. John Gardner wrote an entire book about self-renewing people. In it he makes an observation that is remarkably resonant with so many of our best donors: "One attribute of self-renewing people is that they have naturally fruitful relations with others. They are capable of accepting love and giving it—both more difficult achievements that is commonly thought. They are capable of depending on others and being depended on."

Your donor is your customer.

Think that way. Always think that way.

The best thinking on customer relations applies even more dramatically to donor relations. The concepts of service and appreciation are even more vital to nonprofits than to big business.

Only Rich People Can Help You

MYTH: *If you don't know enough rich people, you can't raise very much money.*

REALITY SHIFT: *The point is not how rich your donor is; the point is how much money he or she leaves you.*

IF SHE WERE A RICH MAN

Carla Turner left one of our organizations $380,000 when she died. This was a shock to us, because she was not known to be a woman of means at all. In fact, she was what most board members would complain of as being a "blue-collar type." But she and her husband worked hard all their lives and saved a little bit every year. Not much, but a little. If you save money from the beginning, you don't have to save very much (or even make very much) to acquire $380,000 over a lifetime of work.

The point is that when Mrs. Turner died, we were her strongest and best relationship on the planet Earth. One of our medical centers had cared for her husband when he was ill, and when he passed away, we continued to stay in close and continuous touch with her because she was a donor and a friend.

The quality and power of the *relationship* with Mrs. Turner was what created the gift of $380,000. It had nothing to do with how rich she was or whether or not she was "blue collar."

We are constantly surprised by the size of gifts we receive from people like Mrs. Turner whose true wealth we had not known about. Our policy is this: Once people give us anything at all, we treat them like kings and queens. We always outgive the giver. We always shift the relationship so that they are continuously thanking *us* for what we have thought to do *for them*. Our staff meetings focus on thanking people and doing thoughtful things for them. We don't try to strike out in new lucrative areas for wealthy new donors; we take care of the donors we have.

By focusing on our donors' commitment to our cause, we have developed relationships that had nothing to do with how rich we thought they were. And they know that! They know that we are grateful to them far beyond their obvious means, because they also know better than anyone that their means are not always obvious.

Many so-called "middle-class" people, especially those who are retired with heirs, end up leaving you surprising amounts of money simply because you had a great relationship with them.

In his introduction to Lautman and Goldstein's classic, Dear Friend: Mastering the Art of Direct Mail Fundraising, David Ogilvy wrote, "I remind you of the 'certain poor widow' who gave Jesus all she had, which was two cents. If her two cents had been invested at compound interest, it would now be worth more than the weight of the world in gold."

MYTH #8

Don't Waste Time on Lawyers and Accountants

MYTH: *Don't waste your time on lawyers, accountants, and other professionals—they don't make good donors.*

REALITY SHIFT: *Whether they make good donors or not, lawyers and accountants are vital to the success of your cause because their clients trust them, and their clients are often your best donors.*

WHO WHISPERS IN THE KING'S EAR?

To get to King Arthur, you must first impress Merlin.

When lawyers and accountants are won over to your cause and become sold on the good works you do, the clients who trust them move a crucial step closer to you.

Lawyers and CPAs work long hours every day to earn the trust of their clients. That trust is so valuable and so hard-won that once it is transferred to you, it is *gold* to your organization.

Advisors to your donors need to know how good your organization is at fulfilling a donor's dreams. They want to feel assured that every dollar given to you by their client *will be used exactly as their client intended!*

So if you have been fanatical about accountability, fulfilling your donors' dreams, and letting them *know* about it, then lawyers, accountants and advisors will say the right things about you when their client looks across the table and asks, "What do you think?" Don't be afraid to keep professionals in the loop. Even if they don't always give a lot themselves (especially when they are young), their influence is worth every ounce of kindness paid to them.

Big Money Comes from Big Companies

MYTH: *Big money comes from big companies.*

REALITY SHIFT: *Statistics show that **less than five cents** of every charitable dollar raised comes from corporations.*

ALL THAT WORK FOR A NICKEL?

If only a nickel of every charitable dollar comes from corporations, how can we justify giving them more than five percent of our time? We can't. Not if we're living in reality. Yet we still see nonprofit organizations spending many wasteful hours chasing after corporate gifts and jumping through the bureaucratic hoops of the corporate application process.

Corporations also have limits, severe limits. They can only give so much, and if their business falls on hard times, they may not be able to give at all next year.

Individual donors do not have such limits. If Microsoft's Bill Gates fell in love with your cause and your organization, what would be the limits on what he could personally give you? His *company* will always have severe limits on what it could donate, but your personal relationship with Bill Gates would know no such limits.

The best thing to do (if you must spend time courting corporations) is to find real live people within those corporations and begin creating relationships with those people as individuals. Concentrate on the *people* more than the corporation. In the long run, the people can help you a great deal more than their companies can.

In addition to how little companies give in the big scope of things, companies often donate to you in order to get something back. To them, a gift is often a way to trade their money for some favorable public relations. And once corporate giving becomes corporate *trading*, you will waste valuable time and human resources keeping corporations satisfied about their PR value per dollar donated.

What would happen if that time and those resources were put into improving your relationships with your best donors?

MYTH #10

You Need a Bigger Staff

MYTH: *You don't have enough staff to raise the money your organization needs.*

REALITY SHIFT: *The number of people you have is not as big a priority as the depth of the relationships you yourself create.*

BUILD IT, AND THEY WILL COME

The popular cry for "More staff!" usually has the cart before the horse. The horse is money raised through relationships. The cart is the staff brought on for thanking.

What truly raises money for you is *not* busy-work done by a large, hyperactive staff. What raises money is the decision made by individual donors to give you very large gifts. That's where your focus should be, on those donors. Once you shift your focus to those donors, you will receive so many financial benefits that adding staff will not be a problem. You'll simply do it as needed, and you'll do it based on whether it will improve relationships with existing donors.

Create enough fruitful relationships, and with the money coming in no one will question you for adding staff as needed. It's trying to add staff *first* that causes you grief, because you think you're in a catch-22 situation when you're not. Preoccupation with size of staff is just another way to distract yourself from the real work that could be done: the person-to-person work that creates long-term, productive relationships.

It all comes back to you. You yourself must begin the financial success of your organization by building relationships of such power and vitality that the gates of donations will open wide. Staff is a reward, not a prerequisite.

ALONE AND AFRAID IN A WORLD
I NEVER MADE

The most popular objection we hear to relationship-building is this: "I don't have time! I'm all alone here! I need more staff. How can I put all that time into developing powerful relationships when I have so many other things to do?"

Okay, fair enough, let's compare it to friendship. How much actual linear time does it take for you to keep a good friendship going? Think now about some longtime good friend from the old days. How much time have you spent with that friend in the past year?

Chances are, your old-time friend doesn't really hear from you very much at all. Yet once you're on the phone together, doesn't something wonderful happen? Don't you feel like you just picked up right where you left off? The same humor, the same bond! Once a relationship is that powerful, it doesn't take that much actual clock time to keep it strong.

You yourself, all alone, can create enough fundraising relationships by concentrating on the quality of exchanges between you and your donors.

Another way to counter the false feeling of not having enough staff is to inspire non-staff people to become a volunteer staff for you. Every person who cares about your organization, with the proper motivation, can become a fundraiser for you. Especially when they learn your system of information exchange and innovative thank-yous. Everyone loves to thank. Once they know you only want them to thank people, you won't have any problem getting volunteers.

Once they learn that they will be helping you *give* to donors (information) and *thank* donors, then they will love working for you, because they no longer have to do the embarrassing work of *soliciting* money.

YOU TELL ME YOUR DREAMS

Here's your mission, on your own, without benefit of staff: Learn to treat your most committed contributors as you would friends, loved ones and family members, so that you can begin to honor their dreams.

The next step is fulfilling those dreams. And in order to fulfill your donor's dreams, you have to know what they are. You have to become an expert on the lives of your donors, especially their inner lives, where the dreams live.

The work done by the money those donors give is what fuels those dreams. Their hearts dance for joy when they realize what they've really done for your cause.

A life's meaning comes from the difference it has made. We are in a unique position to give our donors a way to make a difference in the world. The more we can show them that they have made a difference—the more evidence we can give them of the difference they are making—the happier they will be. They will not want to stop making a difference.

The great philanthropist W. Clement Stone once said, "In giving, I try to multiply myself. I want to change the world and if the institution I'm giving to helps in my objective, then I am multiplying myself in making a gift."

It's your job to help your donors vividly picture the ways in which they are multiplying themselves.

Many fundraisers don't even bother to tell their best supporters where their money went and what it did. As they cry out blindly for more staff, they neglect to do the one thing that would transform donors into major givers.

Especially now in this age of political fundraising scandals and generalized public distrust of all established institutions, prospective donors will be more skeptical than ever about the true destination of their money. But not *your* donors. Because your donors will be continuously surprised with updated information on what their money has done. And your donors will also be surprised by the closeness they feel to your organization . . . a closeness that comes with the innovative thank-yous they get.

Pleasant surprise leads to more giving. Once that giving comes in, you can add staff. Not before. Because if that money is not flowing in, you have yet to master relation-shifting, and without mastering that, adding more staff will just increase the number of people who aren't raising money for you.

You Should Keep Your Communications Simple

MYTH: *In presenting your cause to a prospective donor, keep it simple.*

REALITY SHIFT: *Donors and prospective donors love information about your cause—the more the better. If they are interested in your cause, you should not hold anything back. The more you tell, the more you sell.*

FLY THEM TO THE MOON

If your organization is raising money for space exploration, take your prospective donors as far as you can: let them play among the stars. Give them all the inside information they can handle, and give it to them with a grateful, human touch, with many different people delivering the information in many touching ways.

Many of your donors may have gone to high school forty or fifty years ago. But the truth is that they are still bright and curious (as most successful and financially resourceful people are), so they want to keep learning.

You are in contact with your cause every day. But your donor is not. Your donor yearns to know what you know about your cause.

Successful fundraising professionals deliver more than thank-yous to their donors; they deliver precious inside information.

Lovers of the symphony or the ballet can't get enough positive gossip and inside information about the artists they love to come see. (Ask the artists to write little handwritten letters of thanks. Make them personal and touching.)

Never let someone in your organization thank you for what an influx of money has provided. Whenever anyone thanks you, tell them, "No! It wasn't me. It was our donor. Here is her name and address and phone number. Please thank her. I'll call you next week to see how it went."

Make certain no one ever thanks you. Redirect all thanks to the donor. Appreciation is the deepest craving in human nature. Don't squander any of it, because it is precious to your cause.

Your cause is a passion with your donors, and the more you feed that passion with inside information, the stronger your relationship becomes.

When we give talks for donors to a medical research organization about various aspects of cancer research, we're continually surprised by our donors' wide-eyed love of learning. Such was the case with a man named Claude.

Claude Tomlinson graduated from high school in 1932 in St. Paul, Minnesota. There was little talk back then of chromosomes or genetic engineering. Biology was pretty simple in 1932. Mr. Tomlinson didn't know anything about genetics, even though later in life he made a considerable return on stock investments in biotech companies recommended to him by his broker.

After he gave a moderate gift to our client's research center, we gave him an elaborate laboratory tour and explained, in layman's terms, the advances being made in genetic engineering—advances that were now being sped along by his own contribution.

His boyish fascination with what he was learning was such a delight that staff members began sending him every arcane article they ran across on genetic engineering. (Each article was accompanied by a handwritten note of thanks.) A major relationship was developing—a relationship based on the sharing of inside information.

Although Mr. Tomlinson's initial gift was small, the gifts that followed were not. He later became the research center's largest donor.

Mrs. Mary Bateson had lost her husband and mother to cancer and wanted to do something for cancer research. At that time our client had a pressing need to acquire an important image analysis facility where their researchers could study tumors. Rather than approach Mrs. Bateson with a simple emotional appeal to help our organization's vague and mighty cause, we instead went to work delivering detailed information.

We were relentless in describing the inner complexities of what an image analysis facility would do for us, and how exciting it was going to be to look at tumors and determine ahead of time what the molecular structures of those tumors were.

Note that we weren't talking about a campaign, and we weren't showing Mrs. Bateson a campaign thermometer and telling her how much closer to our goal we'd be if she made a contribution. Instead, we were delivering our product. Knowledge is power in the fundraising business, and we all have an almost infinite amount of knowledge to deliver.

Mrs. Bateson was beginning to understand just what this equipment was going to do for us. She learned that we could begin to examine more closely the chromosomal make-up of tumors, especially for a rare children's brain tumor. We'd even be able to find the molecular change that takes place in neuroblastoma!

Because Mrs. Bateson had contacted us, anxious to make some kind of gift, it would have been easy to get right to discussions on the amount of the gift, the form it would take, etc.

Instead, we absolutely forgot about being "takers" and began *giving* her information about the wonders of our work. It was information she loved learning about, and we enjoyed delivering it.

Once Mrs. Bateson gave the money (more than we ever expected, more than she had originally planned), we sent her the very first chromosome pictures that came off the machine. We don't know whether Mrs. Bateson even graduated from high school, but these esoteric high-tech pictures of chromosomes ended up on her coffee table. It wasn't long before another check came from her for $25,000, absolutely unsolicited.

THE MORE YOU TELL, THE MORE YOU SELL

Don't keep it simple when it comes to information about your cause. Dazzle them with the rich complexity of your mission.

Any time you have an opportunity to provide dramatic inside

information about your cause, seize the opportunity, because it will allow your donor to grow. The human brain stretches every time a new idea enters, and growth is the greatest relationship-builder of all.

Happiness

"Happiness," said William Butler Yeats, "is neither virtue nor pleasure nor this thing nor that, but simply growth. We are happy when we are growing."

The more your donor knows about your cause, the more powerful your relationship is going to be. Don't be afraid to challenge your donor intellectually. It doesn't hurt for him or her to be stretched that way, it feels good.

And don't wait for the proper timing to begin your new information-based relationship with your donors. Start today. Make it happen.

People can be divided into three groups: those who make things happen, those who watch things happen, and those who wonder what happened.

Only the Rich Should Talk to the Rich

MYTH: *Only a millionaire can ask another millionaire for money.*

REALITY SHIFT: *The good-old-boy network is vastly overrated. Your millionaire will give you a major gift because you can make his dreams come true, not because another millionaire asked him for the money.*

OVERRATED PEER RELATIONSHIPS

Development officers have tried over the years to make development a science. They have worked hard to quantify and qualify the kinds of things which seem to be successful in raising money. They've made rules, such as, "Only rich people should call on other rich people."

And certainly it is true that multimillionaires get to know one another. They play golf with each other and trade favors in the business world, and even in the philanthropic world in limited ways. Development officers have always tried to capitalize on those relationships. Even fundraising manuals tell us that we have to form committees of multimillionaires so that they can go out and talk to other millionaires about giving money.

Peer relationships *are* important, but not in the way that the manuals advise—to have your committee's multimillionaire go pressure his peer into giving money.

"Come on, Ed," he is supposed to say. "You asked me to help your organization and I did. Now I'm asking you to help mine."

Please do not ask your committee member to do this! The results will always be limited, and the millionaires will secretly resent the whole process.

There is a better way.

Ask your committee member to introduce his multimillionaire friend to *you*. That's all—no call for money, just an introduction to begin a relationship. Because *you* are the one who needs to have a chance to befriend the other prospect and excite that prospect about your cause. Prospects are much more likely to be charmed by you and your knowledge and contagious enthusiasm than they are by a jocular extortionist golf buddy.

You may not belong to the country club or play golf or tennis, but that does not matter. The prospective donor will not want that from you. *The prospect only wants one thing: to make a difference in this life.* And the limitations inherent in a gift given as a favor-exchange do not exist when you deal with prospects directly. Suddenly all limitations are gone, and you can win as much of their hearts as you are able.

Favor-trading among rich people is here to stay, and it will always raise consistent limited money when the peer pressure is continuously applied. But it will never be the home run your organization is looking for. (Major gifts will grow your organization in dramatic leaps and bounds. Small donations will hardly keep it alive.)

There is another curious aspect to this myth of millionaires needing to ask other millionaires for money. It lies in our perception of a millionaire. It used to be that a "millionaire" meant a Rockefeller or an Andrew Carnegie. It used to mean Donald Trump or Bill Gates or the Queen of England.

Today's millionaires are more like Mr. and Mrs. David Steiner.

The Steiners are from the northwestern United States, where they operated a True Value hardware store for many years. Upon the sale of their home and hardware business, they moved to Arizona. The sale of their home and business netted them over a million dollars in cash. They immediately put the money away. The Steiners then bought an attractive but modest home in a retirement community near a major medical center because they had not been in the best of health.

When we first met the Steiners, it became clear that they wanted to leave a substantial portion of their estate to the organization we were working with. People recommended that we follow the old fundraising myth and find a millionaire to contact the Steiners to complete the talk about the gift.

But these were people who had worked in a hardware store. They weren't fancy country-club types, and sending a millionaire out to meet them was simply an absurd idea. So we continued the relationship as it had started, with the regular, modest staff members visiting with the Steiners. They were the ones who had built the relationship to begin with.

All communications went smoothly and our client's organization was given more than half a million dollars.

The old Joe E. Lewis joke line has a new meaning with the growing number of hardworking, basic, simple millionaires in our society. "It doesn't matter if you're rich or poor," said Lewis, "as long as you've got money."

MYTH #13

Giving Is Purely Emotional

MYTH: *Giving is a purely emotional act.*

REALITY SHIFT: *Giving is only half emotional. The other half is intellectual. The intellectual aspect of giving is the most important half because it is the most neglected.*

THINK AND GROW RICH

In giving, the heart provides the impulse, but the intellect provides the light. The intellect of your donors backs up their heart's impulse with the light of reason. The mind and brain provide the factual reassurance that your cause is a perfect way for the donor to make a difference.

Challenging and stimulating your donor's intellect is yet another way of taking your relationship to a higher level. By bringing your donors into your organization and stimulating them with facts, figures, stories, illustrations, hands-on activities, tours, meetings with top people, conversations, long letters, innovative thank-yous, friendships, trust, and sincere requests for dialogue, you are giving them a way to live their dreams, and a way to grow intellectually.

THE WORDS APPEARED IN *BLOOD*

Mrs. Harvey Johnson lived in Omaha, Nebraska, and had lost her son a number of years ago to lymphoma. She was terribly depressed at the time, as only someone who has lost a child can understand.

Mrs. Johnson was an extraordinarily bright woman who graduated from Columbia University in the class of 1925. She was becoming worried that she had never done anything in memory of her son Robert. When we heard that she was upset about not having memorialized her son, a standard fundraising thought began to occur: This is a typically opportune situation for soliciting a gift!

But that would have been a *taker's* approach. Because we like to operate under the *giver's* philosophy of fundraising, we headed in a different direction. Rather than telling her about all the things our organization could put her son's name on, we began giving her intellectual information about one of the most novel laboratory ideas we had going. We told her about a facility that our research center wanted to put in place, which would lead to answers that no one has ever seen before in lymphoma.

Her $50,000 check bought the new machinery, which was put to work immediately. A year later, out of seventeen patients who were completely drug-resistant and about to die, eight went into remission as a direct result of work funded by her donation.

Did we send her a wall plaque? Did we give her a testimonial lunch? A form letter and a pen-and-pencil set?

No, we went to Omaha with the article that appeared in the obscure hematology journal *Blood*. We showed her the highly scientific article and pointed out that we'd acknowledged her on page 92.

"I'm going to be honest with you, Mrs. Johnson," our staff member told her. "This isn't going to make you famous, because no one reads this journal but hematologists. But there are, quite frankly, eight people who are walking around the world today who would not be alive if it weren't for you."

We weren't quite accurate about one thing—it isn't just hematologists who read that journal. Not any more. *Blood* had found a new subscriber in Mrs. Harvey Johnson.

ALWAYS TRANSFER THE GRATITUDE

After our gentle work behind the scenes, three of the eight people wrote handwritten letters to Mrs. Johnson. Originally, they had tried to thank their doctors, but we have trained our patients and doctors always to transfer the gratitude to the donor, where it belongs.

Every six months or so the medical research center receives another $25,000 from Mrs. Johnson.

You might be thinking, "Well, that's great, but what if you're raising money for a cause that isn't nearly so intellectually exciting as that?"

But think about this more carefully. What great cause does not save lives? There is a popular T-shirt being worn in the arts district of downtown Tucson that says, "Art Saves Lives."

There is no good cause that is not in its own way profound and lifesaving. And there are Mrs. Johnsons connected to every one of your organizations, just waiting for you to travel up to their homes to bring them the latest dramatic and complex intellectual proof of your organization's great work. You can use your own intellect every day to draw parallels to Mrs. Johnson and the work you do.

Once you see the power of the intellect in fundraising, your mission will be to make giving to your organization the means by which your donor makes a greater contribution to the world. You also have the exciting opportunity of making giving to your organization the means by which your donor is enriched intellectually.

Donors find it inspiring when they meet the brightest people connected to your cause. You can have them learn about some of the problems you're trying to conquer, and become intellectually involved in the solving of those problems.

Intellectual enrichment is a gift *we* give. With imagination, we can see that we have an unlimited supply of it. We can walk into our office tomorrow and start giving right away.

Your Board Is Undermotivated

MYTH: *My board of volunteers is not motivated enough to raise the money we need.*

REALITY SHIFT: *Your board is very motivated. They simply haven't been given the proper marching orders.*

LET THE SAINTS GO MARCHING IN

Your volunteers would not be with you if they were not—deep down—very motivated. If they appear to be undermotivated, the problem might be you, not them.

If your board is appearing to be undermotivated, you are probably asking them to do things that throw them right into the "taker" mode and mindset. A very depressing mindset. No wonder they are under-motivated. You would be too!

It's time for a shift. It's time for the board members' thinking to change from taking to giving, from money to relationships, from solic-itation to acknowledgment and gratitude.

Once you have reordered their thinking, so that they are no longer Robin Hoods (trying to take from the rich and give to the poor), they will march for you. Once they've been trained in the art of memorable, personal thank-yous, gratitude lunches, information sharing and rela-tionship building, they will eagerly march for you.

Fundraising doesn't come naturally for most board members. It puts them into an embarrassing position. No wonder attendance at board meetings is a problem! No wonder enthusiasm is missing. Who wants to be a solicitor?

The good people on your board originally thought they would be *giving* a little bit of themselves and their time to join the board of your worthy organization. They probably thought they would be giving a lot of themselves just by showing up for the meetings!

They might even have come to you ready to volunteer to do some work. That's why they looked motivated at the start. They were seeing themselves as givers. They weren't really looking forward to going out and begging their business associates, friends and relatives for money.

When that first discussion of "development" comes up at the board meeting, you can see the board members beginning to grow uncomfortable. They are looking down, or looking around the room, wishing they were anywhere else but there.

How do we remove that discomfort and get these people marching for us? Maybe it's not just marching orders they need: maybe it's the right music, too.

STARS AND STRIPES FOREVER

The marching music that will get your board members going is the music of personal pride. Your board member has to be so proud of the way your organization thanks its donors that he can't wait to bring a new donor in, so he can sit back and watch that donor's surprise and gratitude at the way he is being treated by you and your staff.

Your board members need to see, firsthand, how well you take care of your donors. That's your first job with a new board member.

Your board members also need to be armed with all sorts of great information about your organization to show off. (Not slick brochures, but rather big piles of information and lots of word-of-mouth stories about the good your people do.) They need to understand that you are not asking them to be arm-twisters or money-takers—you are asking them to help you thank people, that's all!

What board member can resist that?

Your board members will then be contacting donors and telling them about the great forces that were set into motion by the donors' gifts. They will be thanking donors and telling them, "That was a wonderful program you created for us, Mrs. Johnson!"

If your board member is a noteworthy person in the community, his thanking activity will be even more effective. Donors will get to say to their friends and family members, "You'll never guess who called *me* today!"

When your board member visits a donor to thank the donor for a gift, he comes back to the next board meeting filled with excitement.

This is a very satisfying process. They did not have to ask for anything at all.

Now, after a number of experiences like that, with board members sharing in the pride of the organization and feeling the glow of thanking people, how are they going to talk about your organization to their wealthy friends and associates?

The truth is they can't *wait* to get their friends involved, because they can't wait to have their friends thanked the way your organization thanks people. They know that ultimately their friends will thank *them* for bringing them on board.

That's why it's important continually to report to your board on all the innovative and thoughtful ways in which you've thanked your donors and delivered vital information to them. You will constantly be reporting to your board about an acknowledgment philosophy that is so thorough and inspiring that your board member can't wait to bring friends and acquaintances into your system. You will read letters from grateful donors to your board. Your board will always see you over-delivering on your promises to donors.

Your goal is not to persuade your board members to go out and raise money. *Your goal is to infect your board members with the excitement of the relation-shift process.* Your goal is to bring your board members closer and closer to the magic of your work and turn them into zealots for your cause.

One great way to do that is to make sure that your board meetings always have a special appearance by someone who is there to thank *them* for the difference your cause has made. Let a grateful recipient of the service you perform thank the board. It really is touching for your board to hear firsthand how the work of the organization is really improving lives.

Once board members become deeply committed to the success of your cause, they will want to help that cause. They will be dying to help that cause in any way they can.

Your only two missions with your board members are (1) to deepen their commitment to your organization, and (2) to allow them to do a lot of thanking.

You will strengthen your relationship with your board members the same way you strengthen your relationship with your donors: through enthusiastic information-sharing. You'll be sharing information about your organization's work and the people you touch.

It is also vital to let your board members develop friendships with the people who do your organization's best work. You will be pleasantly surprised at the sense of team unity that follows.

Remember that your board will perform for you, but only if the music you play for them is right. You want them dancing with delight. The *last* dance you want to ask them to do is the arm-twist.

You Shouldn't Appear To Be Too Successful

MYTH: *It's harmful to your cause for your organization to appear to be too successful.*

REALITY SHIFT: *The best high-profile fundraising organizations continue to raise the most money.*

FLY WITH THE EAGLES

Most donors would rather fly with the eagles than walk with the turkeys. Success breeds success in fundraising. So don't try to hide it.

Johns Hopkins University year after year continues to raise record-setting amounts of money. Why? Because they need it? No. *Because they deserve it and have earned it!*

People continue to support Johns Hopkins *because* there is so much success in what they do, not in spite of it. People like to associate with a winner. People like to join the hunt.

LET YOUR LITTLE LIGHT SHINE

Does this mean that donors won't support you *until* you are successful? No. Not if you are already behaving as if you were success-bound. It's your winning attitude that they will be attracted to.

Yet, most fundraising only gets passionate and energetic when it's desperate. Most groups don't put their hearts and souls into raising money until the group's very existence is threatened. "Help us, help us, or we are going to collapse!"

All of the energy and focus that inspires organizations who are about to go under can also be used in good times! You don't have to wait for a crisis to be enthusiastic about creating great donor relationships and raising large amounts of money.

Donors love coming in at the ground floor and helping to launch a major success. They thrill to that air of possibility your organization conveys. That's real difference-making at its most dramatic. They would rather do that than "save" a poorly run organization from ex-tinction. When they step in to "Save the Symphony!" for example, they know deep down that someone else will have to save it again in a couple of years, if not sooner.

The symphony would not have to be saved if it had done its daily work of creating relationships.

Your job is to dramatize your organization's possibilities to your donors. Your donors will love the idea of helping you reach great success and stature as an organization.

Donors love being present at the creation. When they start to feel your own excitement about the future and your dreams for your organization, they will be eager to help you go wherever you want to go.

And if you are already successful, let it show. It will help you attract relationships with people who are also already successful.

MYTH #16

You Need a System for Recognizing Donors

MYTH: *You need a consistent system for thanking donors.*

REALITY SHIFT: *You will want to create a separate thanking approach for each donor based on that donor's personal relationship to your cause.*

MAKE YOURSELF UP AS YOU GO

There are many books that attempt to teach the nonprofit profes-sional how to raise money. They often give advice on writing case statements and creating the methodologies that their organizations should use to acknowledge donors.

They recommend various mass-mailing programs, telephone pro-grams and special recognition programs, the utilization of which is designed to cause you to raise more money. Without such methodolo-gies—these books claim—you simply cannot succeed.

These books are missing an important point. Systems do not raise money. People do.

Charitable gifts come from the relationships you build with charitable individuals.

And charitable individuals only give money to other individuals whom they enjoy and trust.

Therefore it is wasted effort for your organization to construct or endorse any kind of massive, impersonal acknowledgment "program" in the place of a true commitment to build more powerful relation-ships with a few key people who can help you the most.

HOW TO BUILD POWERFUL RELATIONSHIPS

One way to build powerful relationships is by being a good listener. Most fundraising professionals are so anxious to show off their cause and their brochures, and even show off to the donor the way in which his gift will be recognized, that they never take the time to listen to the donor.

But when you listen, you discover gold. Because it is only through *creative listening* that you realize what kind of program your donor is most interested in helping you fund. And it is also through creative listening that you intuit the kind of recognition that will be most meaningful to that particular donor.

Only by listening to the donor will you learn how he would like to make a difference. And only then can you tailor the perfect developmental fit. Creative listening is the most powerful tool you have in creating relationships.

Most organizations lose their precious individual donors' identities in the very way they recognize the donor! From an anxious meeting room a recognition program will emerge, and plaques or wall clocks or golf clubs will be purchased to give to donors who may not have the slightest desire to receive such stuff.

Your organization can become powerful in recognizing its donors by having each recognition be tailored to the personal life of the donor you are thanking.

That unique personal nature of your donor reveals itself to you when you and your people are engaged in creative listening. Creative listeners are the ones who meet with donors for long conversations and depart from the conversation with the donor feeling inspired, refreshed and fulfilled.

Why?

Because the donor has been doing most of the talking!

Creative listeners can really thank a donor because they know a lot of important things about him or her.

"The meeting of two personalities," said Carl Jung, "is like the contact of two chemical substances. If there is any reaction, both are transformed."

THE DAY OF THE DOLPHIN

Mrs. Katherine Shapiro—a good friend of a cause we were working for—was a lover of dolphins. We discovered this one afternoon during the second hour of listening to her talk about her life and hobbies and dreams. Over a year later, while browsing through an esoteric gift shop in Carmel, we discovered a tape of piano music interplayed with dolphins' voices. We remembered Mrs. Shapiro's love of dolphins, so we bought the tape and sent it to her along with a handwritten note telling her how much she has meant to our cause.

The woman was thrilled far beyond what the $9.95 spent on the tape would justify. When she passed away a year later, she left our organization over $175,000.

This is but one of hundreds of examples of the power of the individualized thank-you. A personalized thank-you makes certain that the nature of the thank-you recognizes something unique about the donor. Although we can't say this for sure, we have a suspicion that had we not listened to Mrs. Shapiro on the subject of dolphins and remembered our talk with her, we'd have had to be content forever with her original $500 donation.

Every one of your relationships is unique. Therefore it is unproductive to try to force-fit a big standardized recognition program onto your precious and delicate group of highly individual persons.

Think of your own personal relationships. When you receive a note or gift, isn't it far more touching to get something that is especially connected to you? Something that recognizes a unique part of who you are? That kind of gift always moves us, and we end up genuinely grateful to the giver for how thoughtful the gift was. What made the gift so moving? It acknowledged something about us that makes us who we are.

To build powerful relationships, don't "honor" your donor thoughtlessly (such as with a standardized plaque or wall clock or watch). Honor your donors in a special way that celebrates their unique way of being.

MYTH #17

You Need Special Events

MYTH: *You need special events to raise money.*

REALITY SHIFT: *Most special events are a bigger problem than you need. Most special events take time, money and effort away from relationship-building (where the real money is).*

NIGHTMARE ON EVENT STREET

Most special events take on the major aspect of a nightmare: in the middle of your preparation for them, you begin to pray they are not really happening.

The two things about special events you can't deny are these:

➤ They *cost* money.

➤ They take more time than you predicted.

The second problem—the waste of time—is the most dangerous. Because once you've made your shift away from the old fundraising myths to relationship-building (the fortune-changing relation-shift we are urging you to make), your time becomes your most useful resource.

Think of the Scripps Institute raising ninety-five percent of its money from those twenty-seven donors. *Time* is what they give to those twenty-seven donors.

You may put on your promotional run, or mountain-climb, or car wash, or bake sale, and you may involve two hundred people in your cause for a day. And you may think there is huge value in reaching those hundred (or even two thousand) people in that way.

But those relationships are casual. Those people may have walked up the mountain in your name and received a visor or T-shirt that was provided by your sponsor, who wanted to get his name out. But as far as relationships go, it was merely a fling—not a true marriage.

This is because their participation was only about the event. Your actual overall cause was just an aside. The event was everything. A fling.

Special events that get in the way of relationship-building are not worthwhile.

Are there exceptions? Yes! Some special events are truly special. Some rare ones even make big money. And some others serve as excellent ways to delight existing donors.

But those are rare. So rare. And they take especially innovative and creative planning and execution. They are the exception, not the rule. If one of that type of event already exists as a tradition in your organization, please leave it in. Be grateful. It is the exception.

If you don't have a special event that is the exception, be very wary of trying to start one. Usually special events take about four times the man-hours you estimate when you first plan them. And that is why you should be careful. They usually end up as a diversionary activity, a way for your organization's staff and volunteers to busy themselves on something other than relationships.

And why would they want to do that? Why, if relationships are your greatest source of money, do charitable organizations devote so much of their time and energy to avoiding conversations that lead to relationships?

Because almost no one really wants to *ask* for money. Shakespeare's "neither a borrower nor a lender be" strikes a deep chord in everyone. And fundraising seems to be worse than borrowing; you are asking for the money to be an outright gift. And not just a gift of sugar, or bottled water, or a blanket for the cold, but money.

It would be okay if money were just money, but if we are talking about fundraising success, we are talking about a lot of money—money that is more than money—money that represents that donor's lifework. It's not easy to ask for that.

So in that passion for avoidance, wild schemes are devised: raffles, bake sales, mountain-climbs, dances and balls, fashion shows, and on and on. Almost all of this is created because we are nervous about asking for money, so we try to devise a diversion to make it "worth it." T-shirts. Cakes.

THE SOLUTION IS A RELATION-SHIFT

The solution to this shame-based avoidance that permeates fund-raising, however, is as simple as it is profound. The solution is to build relationships without asking for any money at all.

Once you have powerful relationships created, of *course* you will do your own version of "asking" for money, but it won't feel like "taking." It will be in response to a definite signal that the donor wishes to be more involved, and it will be accomplished in the spirit of giving: the presentation of an opportunity to make an even greater difference. We are not splitting hairs or playing with semantics here. We are talking about a total soul-level shift from taking to giving.

Once you shift into a giving kind of relationship, you won't be so anxious to distract yourself and everyone else with elaborate special events. You'll enjoy your relationships so much, you will want to devote almost all your time to them. *You will realize instinctively when you are wasting your organization's time, because it will feel like time is wasting every time you're doing something that does not strengthen a relationship.*

Time-wasting tires us out much more than productive work does. And when we are fatigued, we become weak and timid—afraid to make bold, innovative thank-yous and heartfelt communications of inside information.

Fatigue makes cowards of us all.
VINCE LOMBARDI

IS IT POSSIBLE TO HAVE
A GOOD SPECIAL EVENT?

Yes, of course! But that's not what this book is about. This book is to warn you about the ninety percent of special events that do your organization more harm than good. This book is about building relationships.

If you absolutely must be involved in a special event, ask yourself these questions:

➤ Is there a way we can use this event to strengthen our existing donor relationships?

➤ Can we organize this event in such a way that it will create excitement and a boost in morale for our board members, staff and existing donors?

➤ Will our event do a good enough job educating the participants and observers (including media) about our organization's real appeal?

➤ Will we be able to convert a meaningful percentage of the event's participants into enthusiasts for the cause (not just enthusiasts for the event)?

➤ Can we organize and supervise the event in a way that ensures the least time drain on our key people?

➤ If the event turns out to harm, in any way, our overall goal of better relationship-building, will we have the courage to eliminate it?

Your Organization Is Too Unusual

MYTH: *Your organization is so unusual that there isn't enough widespread interest in it to attract big money.*

REALITY SHIFT: *The more unusual your cause is, the more loyal your donors will feel.*

THE INVERSE PROPORTION OF PASSION

The more unusual your cause, the stronger the devotion your followers will feel.

If African-Americans made up more than seventy-five percent of our population, would the United Negro College Fund carry the same poignant appeal? Would the words, "A mind is a terrible thing to waste," be such a part of our culture?

The only challenge unique and unusual organizations may have is in the initial locating and identifying of prospective donors. But once you've got your relationships started, your ability to nurture them and keep the passion and devotion strong is actually *greater* than if you were working for a more "popular" cause.

When you feel you have precious few donors to your cause, the operative word is not "few," but "precious."

SUCCESS LEAVES CLUES

The best use of your time as a fundraiser is the study of your successes. Spend time with the supporters who have given you the most money, and study their psychology. Find out for yourself exactly why they gave money to your cause. The longer you study them, the more you will know about how to succeed in building more of them.

Many of the nonprofit organizations we work for are woefully uninformed about their donors. It is no wonder that they have such a hard time raising money—they don't know why they raised any in the first place. They don't know the real appeal of their organization because they haven't listened to their existing donors.

We recently did a study and action plan for a client whose mission was a center for recovery from addictions. We traveled to snowy Wisconsin to do the initial research work, and we were astonished at what we found.

The staff and board talked to us for the first two days about the mission. They described its appeal, how they attract donations to the cause, and what the difficulties were in courting supporters. But in the next two days we interviewed the organization's top donors and were told a different story altogether. In *their* minds the organization had a unique appeal that was almost completely unknown to its staff.

The staff was operating out of what it had assumed must be the reason people gave money to their institution. They thought people simply favored the general idea of getting addicts clean and sober. Of course that was part of it. But what *really* appealed to the donors was the principles of living being taught by the counselors in the center, and the dramatic philosophical transformation in the center's patients. It was the program for life after sobriety that the donors fell in love with. And if that had been emphasized more in fundraising appeals, much more money would have been raised. If the staff had been in the habit of learning from their own donors, they would probably not have needed to hire outside consultants to help cure the ailing program.

We are reminded of what political consultant Joe Shumate said about consultants. "A consultant," he said, "is someone who borrows your watch in order to tell you what time it is."

It won't take you too long to find out how to raise a lot of money if you are willing to learn from your own donors. Let *them* tell you what your unique appeal was to them. It will help you find more people like them and know what to talk to them about.

It Takes Money
To Raise Money

MYTH: *It takes money to raise money.*

REALITY SHIFT: *It takes **relationships** to raise money.*

DON'T CARE TOO MUCH FOR MONEY

B ecause money can't buy you love.
It can buy you expensive gift offers, expensive special events, expensive tours through Europe, expensive mailing lists, expensive brochures and postage, and many other things that are used to stimulate various diversionary activities. But money can't buy you what you need the most: a few good friends.

The most fruitful fundraising activities don't cost any money at all. They are made up of those little intimate phone conversations you have with the people who have already contributed to your organization. They are made up of the visits on a lonely evening to a widow's home. They are made up of the personal, entertaining private tours of your facilities you give to your donor's family from out of town. They are made up of handwritten notes and letters.

Let's return to the example of one's best friend. In order to improve or strengthen your relationship with your best friend, is it necessary to run out and buy him or her a little gift? A pen or a wall clock? Or would one nice long talk be better?

And once you decided to have that talk, would you insist that it be held on a cruise ship touring the Alaskan coast? Or would a nice little family restaurant be okay?

Everyone wants a chance to make a difference in this world. And once they've selected your organization as one of the ways they are going to make a difference, the best thing you can do is to show them how it's actually happening.

DON'T UNDERESTIMATE YOUR DONOR

Recently we were in the audience in Scottsdale, Arizona, to hear a well-known symphony perform. After the intermission and just before the second half of the evening's performance, the orchestra's charismatic and talented conductor stepped to the microphone and delivered one of the most eloquent and moving fundraising talks we'd ever heard.

Alternately humble and proud, the grand old man of music really touched the heartstrings of this upscale audience. The urge to help him was huge—you could feel it in that magnificent hall. We imagined people gathering with the old master after the performance and giving him checks—huge checks—right there on the spot. That was how skillful his unabashed plea for money was.

But instead, we received a mild shock when he concluded his touching plea with these words:

"And so therefore, ladies and gentlemen, I am asking you to help, and, if possible, to help us tonight. In the lobby, as you leave, you'll see a table with entry forms and some very nice ladies to take your money. For ten dollars, you can buy a raffle ticket for a trip to London we're giving away. It is a wonderful trip for two with marvelous accommodations!"

Ten dollars? What a tragically missed opportunity. And sadly, this story is not at all unusual.

The problem is this: People like the symphony conductor *under*estimate their donors' yearning and ability to give. Because they are so embarrassed at even having to ask for money, they try to cushion their own shame with a ridiculous offer. A trip to London?

That was the worst thing the symphony could have done, because it changed the focus from the conductor's eloquent plea for help to the trip to London. For ten dollars a raffle ticket, you win a chance at a trip to London. That's the new focus for everyone in that audience.

So, do you really want to go to London right now? Do you have time to go? And what are the odds of winning? Do you feel like a fool or a greedy lottery addict if you buy up ten tickets? Even though ten tickets would certainly help the symphony more, you don't want to look foolish, so you buy just one (if any at all).

Yet we would be willing to bet that it took money to secure those London trips. And the people who decided to spend that money probably justified it with, "It takes money to raise money."

In her fact-filled and comprehensive book *Successful Fundraising*, Joan Flanagan quotes a survey done by the Independent Sector, a coalition of top nonprofits and grant makers. Think about our poor symphony conductor when you review these startling facts:

➤ Seventy-five percent of Americans reported that they gave money to charities last year.

➤ Thirty-eight percent of Americans say they wish they had given *more* money. (This means out of every ten people who gave to you last year, four *wanted* to give you more money, but you never created the circumstance that would have made that happen.)

➤ Fourteen percent of Americans revealed that they would have given money, *but nobody asked them.*

Given these facts, does it really seem necessary for you to buy trips or trinkets or other things to provide in raffles in order for your fundraising to succeed?

Ironically, what the people in the audience at the symphony *wanted to do most* was help the symphony! They had just heard a stunning performance followed up by eloquent inside information. They didn't want to go to London; they wanted to feel a *part* of that orchestra and get closer to it. They wanted to know more about it and have it become a bigger part of their lives.

What is it really going to cost you to give a donor a real inside look at your wonderful organization? Maybe it means giving the donor a tour behind the scenes. Maybe it means introducing the donor to some people you wouldn't normally think the donor would be interested in knowing. One of the greatest missed opportunities we've ever experienced has come from thinking that the "worker bee" or the service person in our organization isn't polished enough to spend time with an important donor.

Don't wait for the time when you've got a well-rehearsed presentation and a folder full of documents to invite your donor in. That's not what donors really want. Donors want to see with their own eyes how they're making a difference. When donors see the real benefits of their gifts up close, they become even more enthusiastic about the cause.

It doesn't take money to raise money. It takes relationships.

Fundraising Is
A Frustrating Job

MYTH: *Fundraising is a frustrating and thankless job.*

REALITY SHIFT: *Fundraising that is based on the continuous building of relationships is fulfilling and enjoyable.*

THE FIRST WORD IN FUNDRAISING IS "FUN"

Most people see fundraising as a difficult, thankless and extremely unpleasant task. That's because they are living in the old myths: the myths that see fundraisers as takers. The old myths cause you to cry out: How could anybody enjoy twisting people's arms for a living?

But a relation*shift* in fundraising eliminates arm-twisting. In fact, the arm you were twisting in the past is now draped over your shoulder in a gesture of thanks. When you practice relationship-building instead of arm-twisting, your donors thank *you* for all you have done for *them*!

Many of our clients who have raised startling amounts of money after making this shift have called the idea "revolutionary." And while we agree that it is revolutionary in the world of development, the shift in philosophy from taking to giving is not really a new idea. It was always there in the great wisdom of the past. It was there in the karmic "What goes around comes around" or the biblical "As you sow, so shall you reap." It's the very essence of the Golden Rule, which asks you to do unto others as you would have them do unto you.

But applied today in a fundraising context, it becomes a truly revolutionary approach, simply because no one else is doing it. It is revolutionary, too, in the way it overthrows the traditional governing principles of development (as described in the previous nineteen myths).

To continue to live by these myths *will* make your life in fundraising frustrating and miserable. And you will always be battling your way out of the latest financial crisis.

THE LAST WORD IN FUNDRAISING IS "SING"

"We don't sing because we are happy," observed philosopher William James. "We are happy because we sing."

And in that same spirit, Henry David Thoreau, when asked by his students what the way to happiness was, replied, "There is no way to happiness. Happiness is the way."

The way to transforming your life in fundraising is not a series of steps or systems. It consists of an instant act of becoming. The moment you become a giver instead of a taker, you are transformed. Your role in the universe has changed.

Your subconscious mind becomes electrified with the change: it knows you no longer take for a living, you give. And there is power in that change—a power you can feel.

You will have much to do as a giver. Your newly expanded relationships with your donors will keep you very busy. But that will be welcome, because all that time you were subconsciously seeing yourself as an arm-twister, it was likely that you were constantly procrastinating. That procrastination was natural, because it was only human to want to put off—for as long as possible—*taking* someone else's hard-earned money away from them.

The more you bring donors inside your organization to show them the works of your cause, the more enthusiastic you are. The more enthusiastic you are, the greater your work will be, for as Emerson has said, "Nothing great was ever accomplished without enthusiasm."

FROM MAN TO SUPERMAN

George Bernard Shaw, in his play *Man And Superman,* wrote lines that apply very directly to the enthusiastic fundraiser:

This is the true joy in life, the being used for a purpose recognized by yourself as a mighty one; the being a force of nature instead of a feverish little clod of ailments and grievances complaining that the world will not devote itself to making you happy.

* * *

I want to be thoroughly used up when I die, for the harder I work the more I live. I rejoice in life for its own sake. Life is no "brief candle" to me. It is a sort of splendid torch which I have got hold of for the moment, and I want to make it burn as brightly as possible before handing it on to future generations.

SHIFT WORK

So What Do You Do Now?

STEP TOWARD AN EARTHQUAKE

In the beginning of this book we talked about a shift along your fault lines—a shift that would be significant enough to cause an earthquake. In fundraising we call this a relation-shift because it asks that you shift your activities away from all unproductive work and toward relationship-building. You shift from taking to giving.

This shift is mostly internal, because it involves your entire belief system. We outlined the twenty dangerous myths that make up the belief systems of most fundraisers today. Most people who study the relation-shift system and examine its track record for success are willing to abandon those myths forever.

What follows is pure innovation. After shifting to relationship-building as a central focus of operation, fundraisers can imagine their own ways of relating to each individual donor.

Imagination is more important than knowledge.
ALBERT EINSTEIN

Yet despite this internal shift and the imagination it takes to improve your own relationships with your donors, we still get asked for more specifics.

The most common question at the close of a seminar or in the question-and-answer portion of a speech is, "Okay, all this sounds great, so now what do I do?"

For the briefest possible answer to that question, we would quote from the words inscribed on many of the Cromwellian churches of England: "Think and Thank."

Three little words, but they are the heart and soul of how to shift to relationship-building.

Yet most people want more words than three. They want to be told precisely what to do, so that they can "get it right." The problem with this kind of thinking is that it leads to the "scientific" approach that was featured in all the old fundraising books. Relationship-building is not a science; it is an art. The more rules, steps, systems, programs and policies you have, the less chance you have for imagination and innovation.

It all goes back to a single fact: no one knows your donor like you do. We don't. And the old books on fundraising don't either.

The basic principle of this relation-shift is to shift the sense of importance away from yourself toward your donor. The reason relation-shift fundraising works is that it honors the great American philosopher William James's most profound discovery: The most basic human need is not love, or food, or sex, or money, but a feeling of being appreciated! James referred to that need as our "primary human craving."

THE ROPE LADDER TO SUCCESS

Having said all we have about not wanting to provide specific steps, we will do it anyway—but on these conditions: that you not see these steps as being set in concrete; that you see them as steps made of rope—to be rolled up and tossed overboard once you make it to the top. Because the best steps will always be of your own design, not ours.

Step One: Call a meeting of your staff—everyone who works with you on raising money. This meeting will be to talk about your best individual donors. As each donor's name is brought up, you will encourage each staff member to discuss everything he or she knows about that donor. You will enter all new information into that donor's file (if you don't have donor files, go directly to Step Three). No detail on the donor's life and loves is too trivial. (Do not overlook the seemingly unimportant, such as, "she likes to collect figurines of dolphins.") Find out from your staff when the donor was last communicated with. Was it a personal communication or (shame on you by now) an institutional mailing? Who will communicate with the donor next? What kinds of inside information would it be most fun to deliver?

Step Two: Schedule a meeting—away from office interruptions—between you and one member of your staff. This will be repeated until your entire staff has had a one-on-one meeting with you. In this meeting, encourage your staff member to discuss his own interpretation of relationship-building. Ask for suggestions about building more powerful relationships with individual donors. Talk about any reservations the staff member might have about making a complete shift. Then assign that staff person three donors to take under her wing in a special way, and express confidence that she will come up with some very imaginative ways to tighten the connection between those donors and your organization.

Step Three: Select someone who is good on the computer and good with details to become the captain of the donor files. In smaller organizations, this might even be you! And in noncomputerized organizations, a series of index card boxes works marvelously.

Be certain that the manager of the donor files knows that he is the navigator of your organization's journey toward ultimate success! Together, you will agree on what is to be stored in your individual donor database:

➤ Dates and summaries of previous communications with that donor.

➤ Dates and amounts of donor's gifts.

➤ Personal information about the donor and his or her family.

➤ Your donor's dreams for making a difference in the world.

➤ Donor's birthday.

➤ Any other observation you can compile that will heighten your organization's ability to relate more personally and thoughtfully to that donor.

Step Four: Meet personally with each member of your board, and do not discuss raising money unless the board member insists. Instead, discuss:

➤ What you've done this month to thank donors and keep them informed.

➤ What your organization is doing that is exciting and how people are being helped by your organization's work.

➤ How much you appreciate the time already given by your board member to the cause.

Step Five: Make a list of people in your organization who normally do not thank your donors, but who *could* and would if they were asked. Match each one of these people to a particular donor and let them improvise. They can use whatever form of communication they are most comfortable with, but stress how good it would be if that donor came away from the encounter feeling *more important to your cause.*

Step Six: At week's end, set aside an hour to thank the thankers. Make sure that everyone who has been engaged in creating innovative thank-yous and delivering inside information gets acknowledged.

Step Seven: Pick a donor whom you yourself would like to get to know better. Allow yourself to listen to that donor, to learn from him, and to be enriched by the experience.

THROW THE LADDER AWAY

The seven steps recommended above should take you to the next level, especially if relationship-building has not been your focus in the past. But remember that this was a rope ladder, to be thrown away as soon as you reach that plateau.

How high can you eventually go? There is no limit. Americans will give over 200 billion dollars to charity this year, and if they were persuaded that there were good causes they'd give more!

You will persuade them—not just with words, but also by the way you treat them. You can show them something few people can ever show them. You can show them the difference their lives can make.

It's not very difficult to persuade people to do what they're already longing to do.
ALDOUS HUXLEY

About the Authors

MICHAEL BASSOFF is a nationally recognized leader in health sciences development and was named president by the trustees of the Foundation of the University of Medicine and Dentistry of New Jersey (UMDNJ). In this position he is responsible for raising and managing private funds given in support of the University and all of its programs.

Bassoff established a highly successful development program at the University of Arizona Health Sciences Center based largely on securing gifts from private individuals through a broad-based volunteer effort. Having been the first fundraising person ever hired at that center, he spent sixteen years creating a comprehensive development program and an extraordinary relationship between the people of Arizona and the University of Arizona Health Sciences Center. During his tenure at Arizona, the endowment of that University doubled, and the fundraising program became one of the most successful in the western United States. Over the years, Bassoff has worked with dozens of nonprofit organizations ranging from botanical gardens to religious schools. A native of Highland Park, New Jersey, he lives in New Jersey with his family.

STEVE CHANDLER is the author of a number of best-selling books, including *50 Ways to Create Great Relationships* and *Reinventing Yourself.* Chandler is a public speaker and seminar leader who specializes in sales, fundraising, and customer relations. His corporate clients include Intel, Motorola, Wells Fargo Bank, American Express, Texas Instruments, and hundreds of others. He is also a popular speaker and seminar leader in the nonprofit world.

ROBERT D. REED PUBLISHERS ORDER FORM

Call in your order for fast service and quantity discounts.

(541) 347-9882

Or order online at **www.rdrpublishers.com** *using Paypal.*

OR order by mail: Make a copy of this form; enclose payment information:

Robert D. Reed Publishers, P.O. Box 1992, Bandon, OR 97411

Fax: (541) 347-9883

Send indicated books to:

Name _____

Address _____

City _____ State _____ Zip _____

Phone _____ Cell _____

E-mail _____

Payment by check _____ or credit card _____ *(All major credit cards accepted.)*

Name on card _____

Card Number _____

Exp. Date _____ Last 3-digit number on back of card _____

Books by Steve Chandler:

Quantity			Total
_____	*RelationShift: Revolutionary Fundraising*	$14.95	_____
_____	*Ten Commitments to Your Success*	$11.95	_____
_____	*100 Ways to Create Wealth* (with Sam Beckford)	$24.95	_____
_____	*The Joy of Selling*	$11.95	_____
_____	*Fearless*	$12.95	_____
_____	*Shift Your Mind; Shift Your World*	$14.95	_____
_____	*Small Business Millionaire* (with Sam Beckford)	$11.95	_____

Books by the Williams Group (Roy Williams & Vic Preisser)

_____	*Philanthropy, Heirs and Values: How Successful Families Are Using Philanthropy to Prepare Their Heirs for Post-Transition Responsibilities*	$29.95	_____
_____	*Preparing Heirs: Five Steps to a Successful Transition of Family Wealth and Values*	$29.95	_____

Other Books

_____	*Living Your American Dream* (Michael Marciniak)	$12.95	_____
_____	*Straight-Line Leadership: Tools for Living with Velocity and Power in Turbulent Times* (Dusan Djukich)	$27.95	_____

Total Number of Books _____ Total Amount _____

Note: Shipping is $3.50 1ˢᵗ book + $1 for each additional book.

Shipping _____

THE TOTAL _____